D1087890

# SMASHING STIGMA

## DISMANTLING STEREOTYPES, PREJUDICE, AND DISCRIMINATION

### BY CONNIE GOLDSMITH

TF
CB

TWENTY-FIRST CENTURY BOOKS / MINNEAPOLIS

# TRIGGER WARNING

This book contains discussions of depression and suicide, self-harm, addiction and overdose, sexual assault, intimate partner violence, and war. If any of these subjects are traumatizing to you, please skip those chapters.

Twenty-First Century Books™
An imprint of Lerner Publishing Group, Inc.
241 First Avenue North
Minneapolis, MN 55401 USA

For reading levels and more information, look up this title at www.lernerbooks.com.

Main body text set in Avenir LT Pro.
Typeface provided by Linotype AG.

**Library of Congress Cataloging-in-Publication Data**

Names: Goldsmith, Connie, 1945–author.
Title: Smashing stigma: dismantling stereotypes, prejudice, and discrimination / Connie Goldsmith.
Description: Minneapolis: Twenty-First Century Books, [2023] | Includes bibliographical references and index. | Audience: Ages 13–18 | Audience: Grades 7–9 | Summary: "Stigma is everywhere, from mistrust of unhoused people to discrimination based on weight. Discover how to identify and confront stigma and stop the spread of stereotypes, prejudice, and discrimination"— Provided by publisher.
Identifiers: LCCN 2022023691 (print) | LCCN 2022023692 (ebook) | ISBN 9781728477398 (library binding) | ISBN 9781728485959 (ebook)
Subjects: LCSH: Stigma (Social psychology)—Juvenile literature. | Discrimination—Juvenile literature. | Prejudice—Juvenile literature.
Classification: LCC HM1131.G65 2023 (print) | LCC HM1131 (ebook) | DDC 305—dc23/eng/20220527

LC record available at https://lccn.loc.gov/2022023691
LC ebook record available at https://lccn.loc.gov/2022023692

Manufactured in the United States of America
1-52375-50732-2/22/2023

# TABLE OF CONTENTS

# CHAPTER 1

# STIGMA:
# IT'S EVERYWHERE

S tigma is a mark of disgrace associated with a particular
circumstance, quality, or person. It's a false idea that
can lead to negative beliefs about a person's perceived
characteristics, such as a particular behavior or condition. And
it can result in harmful actions. It's in the negative views we
may hold about other people and in our disapproval of things
we don't understand. That lack of understanding can make
another person seem different, untrustworthy, or unstable in
some way.

Stigma is all around us. It's so common we may not even
notice it. It can cause a boy to be too afraid to tell anyone he
sees a therapist for depression. He doesn't want to face the
negative comments people may say about him. "Just snap out

of it," they might say. "Stop feeling sorry for yourself." Or stigma could be directed at people who used to take drugs. They're in recovery, but other people's incorrect belief that "once an addict, always an addict" has made those with addictions feel too ashamed to talk about their experiences. Or it's directed at a girl whose boyfriend abuses her. Stigma prevents her friends and family from understanding that she needs their help, and they may even blame her for "making him angry." And don't stop and talk to that unhoused man—he's probably dangerous!

Stigma can be directed at anyone. Even if you're a highly paid guard in the National Football League (NFL). Brandon Brooks, formerly of the Philadelphia Eagles and the Houston Texans, has been open about his mental illness since 2016. At times, Brooks experiences severe anxiety. The stomach pain, nausea, and vomiting that go along with his anxiety have kept Brooks from playing several football games during his career. In 2019 he had to leave an important game against the Seattle Seahawks just before Thanksgiving.

"Make no mistake, I'm NOT ashamed or embarrassed by this nor what I go through daily," Brooks said in an interview after the game. "I've had this under control for a couple of years and had a setback yesterday. The only thing I'm upset about is that when my team needed me, I wasn't able to be out there with and for them." Like so many people, Brooks faces stigma because of his anxiety. People may say things like, "Stomach pain is going to keep him from playing in an important football game? He's being so dramatic! He should just push through it and play the game."

People may be most familiar with the stigma associated with mental health issues, but it also can arise for other reasons. Addiction, being unhoused, intimate partner violence, race, and even body weight carry their own

Brandon Brooks was one of the first active players in the NFL to speak out about mental health. Many sports fans believe that Brooks's football legacy should be as much tied to his openness about mental health as his plays on the field.

stigma. Stigma and its results seriously affect the well-being of those who experience them and can change how people feel about themselves. Stigma can affect people when they are having problems, while they are in treatment, and even years later. It's hard enough to deal with a serious issue in your life. You want to count on help from your friends and family. But that isn't always possible. Being stigmatized for your struggles makes them even more difficult to overcome.

## STIGMA, STEREOTYPES, PREJUDICE, AND DISCRIMINATION

To reiterate, stigma is a mark of disgrace associated with a quality or behavior, or the negative beliefs that someone holds about another person who has particular traits or characteristics. Stigma produces inaccurate beliefs against people who may have certain conditions or display behaviors that others see as strange or wrong. The negative beliefs of stigma lead to stereotypes. They can lead to prejudice and then to discrimination and the denial of human rights that every person deserves.

People may stigmatize the same trait to different degrees depending on how much they know about it or what the cause of the behavior is. For example, if someone stumbles over their words because they suffered a stroke, others may not stigmatize that behavior. But if a person is stumbling over words because they have an alcohol addiction and are intoxicated, they may experience more stigma. Other people may believe that person should be able to stop drinking and that the addiction is the person's own fault.

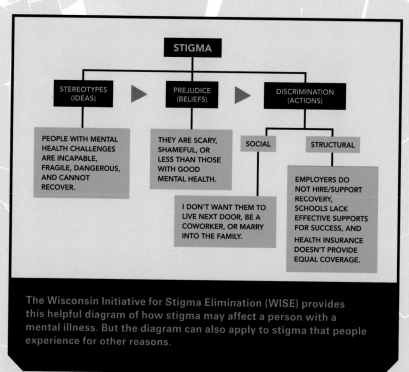

**STIGMA**

STEREOTYPES (IDEAS)

PREJUDICE (BELIEFS)

DISCRIMINATION (ACTIONS)

PEOPLE WITH MENTAL HEALTH CHALLENGES ARE INCAPABLE, FRAGILE, DANGEROUS, AND CANNOT RECOVER.

THEY ARE SCARY, SHAMEFUL, OR LESS THAN THOSE WITH GOOD MENTAL HEALTH.

SOCIAL

STRUCTURAL

I DON'T WANT THEM TO LIVE NEXT DOOR, BE A COWORKER, OR MARRY INTO THE FAMILY.

EMPLOYERS DO NOT HIRE/SUPPORT RECOVERY, SCHOOLS LACK EFFECTIVE SUPPORTS FOR SUCCESS, AND HEALTH INSURANCE DOESN'T PROVIDE EQUAL COVERAGE.

The Wisconsin Initiative for Stigma Elimination (WISE) provides this helpful diagram of how stigma may affect a person with a mental illness. But the diagram can also apply to stigma that people experience for other reasons.

1. *Stereotypes.* Stigma puts individual people who may have similar traits into groups and makes anyone who has those traits part of a stereotype. Stereotypes are oversimplified and mistaken ideas about a group of people based on how they look or act. For example, a person may believe a stereotype that says people with mental illnesses are fragile, incapable of caring for themselves, and even dangerous. Or a stereotype can be as simple as "people who wear glasses are smart" or "athletes are tough."

2. *Prejudice.* This refers to preconceived and negative beliefs about groups of people who fit a stereotype, such as those with a mental illness, or those of a different race or religion from your own. For example, a Muslim girl who wears a hijab may face prejudice in the United States. Perhaps someone holds incorrect beliefs that all Muslims are dangerous or somehow anti-American. The prejudice is against Muslims, rather than against that particular girl. People can experience prejudice for other reasons, such as against people who have an addiction or are unhoused.

3. *Discrimination.* This is any action taken against people based on the stereotypes and prejudice against them. It can include behaviors such as refusing to live near or work with someone different from you. For example, employers who haven't recognized or addressed the stigmas they may hold in their own lives can discriminate when they don't hire someone they perceive as being too different, whether it be someone with a mental illness, a person of color, or someone recovering from an addiction.

Stigma causes prejudice and discrimination, the harmful thoughts and acts against anyone perceived as different. For example, the National Alliance on Mental Illness (NAMI) says that stigmatized people are often

- alienated and seen as "others,"
- perceived as dangerous,
- seen as irresponsible or unable to make their own decisions,
- less likely to be hired,
- less likely to get safe housing,
- more likely to be criminalized than offered health care services, and
- afraid of rejection to the point that they don't always pursue opportunities.

Seeing a therapist may help people who feel stigmatized. The insight they gain may help them educate people who are displaying stigma against them. It may help to know that we are all more alike than we are different. And people who become aware they are holding stigmas against others can benefit by recognizing it, talking about it, and reading about it. Decreasing stigma is an outcome most people would like to see—whether they are on the giving or the receiving end.

## GROWING UP WITH STIGMA

Millions of people of every age experience stigma and discrimination each day. According to the World Health Organization, mental illness affects one in seven people ages ten through nineteen. So, in a classroom of thirty young people, at least four of them are likely to have a mental illness. Each of those students might feel alone or different because of the stigma they face every day.

# STIGMA IN ATHLETES

Brandon Brooks isn't the only athlete to go public about his mental health. Top tennis pro Naomi Osaka and Olympic medalists Simone Biles and Michael Phelps have all spoken out about their mental health in recent years.

Simone Biles was presented the Presidential Medal of Freedom in 2022 for her advocacy for athletes' mental health and safety as well as children in foster care and victims of sexual assault.

Osaka dropped out of the French Open tennis tournament in 2021. She cited her mental health as the reason, revealing on Instagram that she'd struggled with depression and anxiety for years. Osaka said, "I think now the best thing for the tournament . . . and my well-being is that I withdraw so that everyone can get back to focusing on the tennis going on in Paris." She wrote in the *New York Times*, "It's O.K. to not be O.K."

Biles, who won seven Olympic medals in 2016, withdrew from gymnastic competition in the Tokyo Olympics in 2021. She was experiencing "the twisties," a dangerous condition in which gymnasts lose awareness of where they are in the air during a routine. Stressed and anxious, Biles made the right decision for herself. "At the end of the day, we're human, too, so we have to protect our mind and our body rather than just go out there and do what the world wants us to do," she said.

Phelps, who won twenty-eight Olympic medals during his swimming career, has disclosed that he struggles with depression and anxiety. "I stuffed my emotions away because I couldn't show that weakness or that vulnerability," Phelps said. "As an athlete, it's challenging, especially for a male. We're supposed to be big and strong and macho, not somebody who struggles with their emotions." He applauds what Biles did. He said, "[Biles] opening up and talking about mental health is a big, powerful step forward toward blowing the stigma out of the water."

When publicly renowned athletes such as Brooks, Osaka, Biles, and Phelps openly discuss their mental health challenges, it helps to reduce the stigma of mental health issues for everyone.

Young people with mental health conditions are especially vulnerable to social exclusion and discrimination by their peers. Their classmates may avoid them or bully them for their mental illness. This can lead to difficulties with classwork, poor physical health, and risk-taking behaviors such as using drugs or drinking alcohol, getting into fights, and unsafe driving.

When parents, teachers, and other caring adults offer support to troubled teens, that can make a big difference. Without help, the ongoing stigma that some young people live with can become a cycle of self-hate. People who experience stigma often internalize it—they come to believe the distorted beliefs others have about them. Internalizing stigma causes feelings of distress, shame, and hopelessness. It can make someone think, "I am not good enough." The person may wonder, Why bother to fight back? Why should I try to change other people's opinions of me?

Stigma makes people feel alone, even if they're surrounded by others who are experiencing similar feelings. Stigma can lead people to think less of themselves or to hate who they are—sometimes leading to self-harm or wanting to take their own lives. As award-winning author and certified mental health therapist Chris Crutcher says, "One thing people often fail to understand is that kids who have experienced stigma and discrimination tend to believe there is something wrong with *them*. They may feel as if perpetrators of that mistreatment knew what was wrong. Therefore, the abusers were justified in their abuse."

Some people must deal with more than one kind of stigma. One of those people, e.E. Charlton-Trujillo, is the prize-winning author of the *Fat Angie* trilogy, filmmaker, and advocate for troubled young people. "I was an adopted Mexican-American in a mostly racist Caucasian family in a

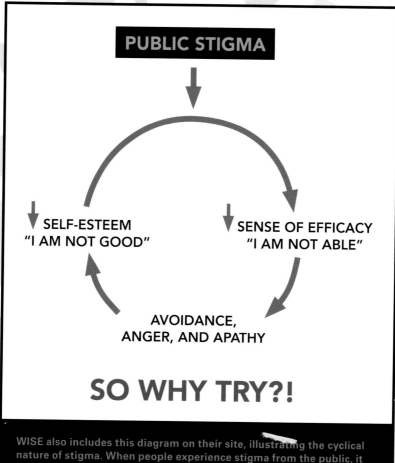

**PUBLIC STIGMA**

SELF-ESTEEM
"I AM NOT GOOD"

SENSE OF EFFICACY
"I AM NOT ABLE"

AVOIDANCE,
ANGER, AND APATHY

## SO WHY TRY?!

WISE also includes this diagram on their site, illustrating the cyclical nature of stigma. When people experience stigma from the public, it lowers their belief in themselves. They may feel angry or apathetic or may try to avoid others. Their self-esteem lowers, and the cycle continues.

small south Texas town. The family was violent and riddled with drug and alcohol addiction yet presented itself to the world as all-American. I was a queer kid filled with self-loathing because of my sexual orientation," Charlton-Trujillo says of the multiple stigmas they faced as a child.

They will always remember what happened one Friday afternoon when they were thirteen:

A basketball hit me in the head during practice. I blacked out but shook it off and rode with my team to watch an out-of-town game. On the bus ride home, I had a seizure. I couldn't remember what happened, but my coach told me.

Back at school on Monday morning, gossip festered in the hallways—stories of the maybe queer kid who was a freak show. It turned out I had epilepsy, but my father said not to talk

## A THERAPIST'S EXPERIENCE

Ann Steiner, PhD, is a psychotherapist and author. Steiner says, "Sadly, stigma is alive and well, and it's everywhere. It could be about the girl who struggles with her invisible pain and doesn't want her friends at school to know. Or it could be about my patient who has psoriatic arthritis—a painful condition with rashes all over the body. His friends shy away from him as if he might be contagious." She explains:

Stigma comes in many forms. I frequently see adults who were traumatized by being bullied when they were teens. Bullying happens most often to children and teens who appear different, or who have low self-confidence. For example, Charlie had some learning challenges when he was young and wanted to be accepted by his classmates. He talks about the long-lasting impact of being bullied in elementary school. The popular boys surrounded Charlie and beat him up almost every day after school. He learned "to be nice" to bullies, hoping they would stop picking on him, and let him join their circle. To this day, despite being successful in his chosen about it. Worse than the disease itself were the cruel stories that kids and their parents made up. How I had AIDS. Used drugs. Was possessed. Nasty letters left in my locker. Phone calls not returned by friends. Places I was no longer welcome.

The stigma of an illness I couldn't control became my identity. And the loneliness and isolation sunk me into a depression and a spiral of self-harm. When someone isolates

work, Charlie struggles with being hard on himself.

Another place where I see stigma in action is with people who have chronic medical issues or disabilities. Teens are often naturally self-conscious and don't want to be seen as different. A few thoughtless, insensitive, or hurtful words can be remembered for a lifetime. Harsh words can trigger painful memories and feelings of inadequacy. The challenge then is to see that we are not defined by our limits but by what we do with them. When I listen to my patients talk about the emotional pain that can return so quickly, it reminds me of the power of words to both hurt and heal.

Most of us feel different or that we don't belong some of the time. But many of the people I work with feel that way most of the time. It continues to surprise me that in this day and age there is still stigma about people going to therapy: "You must be crazy to go to therapy!" Really? You wouldn't want a loved one who's in emotional or physical pain to learn how to cope with it? That's what therapy is.

what is perceived as different in a person and amplifies it with ridicule and cruelty, invisible wounds can pierce far into the body. It settles deep inside of who and what the targeted person thinks they are at their core. And that . . . that is dangerous.

Charlton-Trujillo explains how other stigmas can affect young people. They say, "Stigmas related to homelessness, poverty, body image, mental health, race, religion, neurodiversity, illness, and being LGBTQIA+ can create youth who are at risk of not meeting their full potential. Stigmas act as barriers, making it difficult for young people to accurately see themselves. We need to avoid stigma around perceived or actual differences and recognize the power in our personal stories."

Stigma and the resulting discrimination make life even more difficult for people who already face challenges. Combating stigma is a major step toward greater understanding and connection between all of us.

## THE CONSEQUENCES OF STIGMA

The results of stigma are dangerous. Stigma is harmful because it leads to stereotypes, which do not allow people to think about a stigmatized individual's personal experience. That in turn leads to prejudice, where individuals are ostracized or judged based on the stereotype they are forced into. Finally, prejudice leads to discrimination, when the stigmatized individual is denied rights that every person deserves. Stigma sets in motion a downward spiral with an uncertain ending.

Stigma and the resulting effects can seriously damage people's well-being, especially children and teens. As Crutcher says, "The stigma that badly treated children live with plays out badly for them, partly because how they see themselves is often the way other kids see them. It's kind of like a snake eating its own tail." Some children will have difficulty coping with stigma and its results as they grow up. But many, such as Charlton-Trujillo, use those experiences to help others when they become adults. If everyone makes an effort to understand and address their own preconceived notions, we can all reduce harmful stigma. This book aims to show you how six common types of stigma arise and how you can address them in your own life. These are not the only types of stigma, but they should provide examples of how it may manifest and impact those around you.

# CHAPTER 2

# I'M NOT CRAZY: LIVING WITH THE STIGMA OF MENTAL ILLNESS

**B**eing a teen is hard. You face a lot of stress that can make you anxious or depressed. You want to do well in school. You want to get along with your family and friends. You want to make the right decisions for your future. Will you get a job or go to college? Where will you live? How will you know when you find the right partner? And living through a history-making pandemic made everything more difficult. It's normal to feel stressed or worried about the pressure that comes your way. But how much is too much?

## WHAT IS GOOD MENTAL HEALTH?

Maintaining your mental health is just as important as maintaining your physical health. It's pretty easy to know if you're in good physical health. But it's a little trickier to gauge your mental health. We all have ups and downs. We all get worried or angry. We feel sad over a breakup and frustrated about a tough day at work or school. Are those signs of mental illness? Probably not.

So how do you know if you have good mental health? Young people with good mental health show many of the following qualities. Most of the time they

- feel good about themselves and enjoy life,
- can cope with stress and disappointment,
- have good relationships with family and friends,
- eat a healthy diet and get enough exercise, and
- feel that they belong and that their lives have meaning and purpose.

It would be wonderful if we all felt like this all the time. But that's not realistic. It's normal to be sad, anxious, angry, stressed, or depressed—some of the time. So what is the difference between normal and not so normal?

## WHAT IS MENTAL ILLNESS?

NAMI is the nation's largest grassroots mental health organization dedicated to building better lives for the millions of Americans that mental illness affects. The organization strives to promote hope for people who have a mental illness by fighting for equitable treatment for all people regardless of their background and educating the public about mental health. NAMI says that half of all mental health conditions have begun by the age of fourteen, while three-fourths have started by the age of twenty-four. Unfortunately, many cases of mental illness go unrecognized and untreated. Without treatment, mental health conditions that develop in adolescence may extend into adulthood.

## AMANDA'S STORY

In 2012 Amanda Lipp became the youngest director to have ever served on the NAMI board in California. She has since served on multiple boards for mental health organizations. But she had to overcome serious mental health problems to accomplish these feats. Lipp often shares her story with young people during meetings and presentations. She says, "I was in constant therapy and on medication the last two years of high school. Yet I still had a mental breakdown my freshman year of college and was hospitalized for three months. It goes to show that even with resources and a supportive network, things can still go wrong."

Amanda explains:

Group therapy didn't work for me. Individual therapy didn't work either. Now therapy does work, but when I was at my worst—my most suicidal time—nothing worked. I had to hit rock bottom to realize what I had to lose. The turning point was when a psychiatric nurse handed me a box of crayons and I began expressing myself with them. Art became a medium to translate my dark thoughts into hopeful ones. This gave me the confidence to tell my story to my care team, and later, when I was discharged, to share my story publicly. This helped me personally, and also helped me find community.

When I began to acknowledge my identity and to see adverse experiences as *opportunities* to grow and diversify, I noticed a change within myself and how others viewed me. People started to treat me in the same way I had evolved to view myself—with respect and pride. It's easier said than done, but with support, this helps to reverse the cycle of stigma and cultivates empathy.

I see less stigma about mental illness among young people than there was just ten years ago. Social media, technology, and more knowledge about mental health has changed everything. For example, education and resources have allowed LGBTQIA+ people to come out more easily. Now kids are identifying in many different ways because they feel free to do so. They have the liberty and freedom to love whoever they want. Education has finally caught up to humanity to allow people to express themselves and to share their story.

This is one of the art pieces Lipp created as part of her therapy. She calls this crayon drawing *Unmasked Self*.

It's important to know when normal behavior becomes a mental health issue. According to NAMI, some of the warning signs of possible mental illness include

- feeling very sad or withdrawn for more than two weeks;
- engaging in risky behavior that may harm yourself or others;
- feeling sudden overwhelming fear for no reason;
- gaining or losing a significant amount of weight;
- seeing, hearing, or believing things that aren't real;
- excessively using alcohol or drugs;
- experiencing drastic changes in mood, behavior, personality, or sleeping habits; or
- feeling intense worries or fears that get in the way of daily activities.

If you or someone you care about is experiencing these changes in behavior, talk to a trusted adult—a parent, guardian, teacher, counselor, doctor, or family friend. NAMI offers a free help line at (800) 950-6264. Volunteers answer questions, offer support, and discuss next steps you could take. Or you can ask to speak to a trained crisis counselor. Suicide is the second-leading cause of death for people between ten and twenty-four. If you suspect someone is thinking about suicide—or if you are—call the Suicide and Crisis Lifeline at 988 or (800) 273-8255. Help is available 24/7.

## WHAT ARE SOME COMMON MENTAL ILLNESSES?

Anxiety disorders are the most common mental health conditions in the United States. At least 7 percent of people aged seventeen and under struggle with anxiety. Most people who have an anxiety disorder develop the disorder before they turn twenty-one. But what's the difference between the normal anxiety most of us feel some of the time and an actual mental health concern?

People dealing with too much anxiety may experience a pounding heart, shortness of breath, and headaches. Their hands may shake. They're likely to be fearful, jumpy, and irritable, and they may expect the worst to happen in any situation. Mental health experts diagnose several kinds of anxiety, such as phobias—an unreasonable fear of something. Some people may have a phobia of flying, being in crowds, or running into spiders or clowns. Anxiety and phobias can lead to panic attacks, or sudden feelings of debilitating terror and anxiety. During a panic attack, people may struggle to breathe and experience intense chest pain and dizziness. Up to 11 percent of Americans have experienced a panic attack.

Depression is also common among adolescents and adults. Everyone feels depressed sometimes, but occasional depression is not a mental illness. Severe depression can make people feel as if their lives don't matter. It can lead to changes in sleep and appetite, loss of energy and concentration, aches and pains, lack of interest in favorite activities, feelings of worthlessness and guilt, and even suicidal thoughts. Many things can cause depression, including a change in life circumstances, such as a death in the family, a serious illness or other physical problem, and drug or alcohol abuse.

Bipolar disorder is a condition where people experience extreme highs and lows. People with bipolar might compare it to a never-ending ride on a roller coaster that constantly goes up, up, up, and then plunges down, down, down. The highs are called mania, and the lows are episodes of depression. Some people may not experience symptoms for years, while others cycle through their episodes of mania and depression more often. During a manic period, people with bipolar are hyperactive and impulsive, and they sometimes make bad decisions. Periods of depression can be debilitating, bringing constant feelings of guilt, helplessness, and failure. But some people may not experience depressive episodes. Others might experience hypomania, a less severe form of mania. Psychotic episodes—hearing and seeing things that aren't real—can occur with either mania or depression. An estimated 4.4 percent of adults in the US have experienced bipolar disorder at some time in their lives, often during their teen years. Scientists have not yet found a cure for bipolar disorder. But with therapy and the right medications, most people with bipolar disorder can live normal, productive lives.

Obsessive-compulsive disorder (OCD) affects over two million Americans. The average age of onset is nineteen, but it can begin by the age of fourteen. People with OCD experience irrational fears or obsessions that lead to compulsions—strong drives to do things that are not normal. They may worry about dirt and germs and feel compelled to wash their hands dozens of times a day. They may feel the need to line things up in a certain order, such as canned goods in the kitchen or toys on a table. People with OCD may fear they forgot to lock the door and keep checking to be sure over and over. Some people do not give in to their compulsions, but for many people with OCD, the overwhelming fear of a negative consequence, such as their house burning down if they don't check to make sure the oven has been turned off again, makes the compulsion incredibly difficult to ignore.

Schizophrenia is a mental disorder in which people interpret reality abnormally. It may result in a combination of hallucinations, delusions, and extremely disordered thinking and behaviors that impair daily functioning. Schizophrenia

## WORDS MATTER

Even if your heart is in the right place, your words may be unintentionally harmful. Think about what you say. A person is not their disease. Someone is not bipolar but instead is a person with bipolar disorder. A person is not schizophrenic but a person with schizophrenia. This concept applies to more than mental health disorders. People are not addicts; they have addictions. People are unhoused, rather than homeless. And people commit crimes; they do not commit suicide. Instead, you can say someone took their own life or they died by suicide. If someone talks to you about their condition in a certain way, do your best to honor their knowledge and preferences in the words they choose to use.

can be disabling. Early treatment may help get symptoms under control and improve the long-term outlook. People with schizophrenia require lifelong treatment. Men often experience the first symptoms of schizophrenia in their late teens or early twenties, while women tend to show the first signs of the illness in their twenties and early thirties.

Esmé Weijun Wang, an award-winning author, has lived with schizoaffective disorder—a disorder that causes symptoms of schizophrenia combined with symptoms of bipolar disorder—for much of her life. After she was hospitalized for mental illness in college, the school officials asked her to leave. "Rather than receiving help, mentally ill students are frequently, as I was, pressured into leaving—or ordered to leave—by the schools that once welcomed them," she wrote in her book, *The Collected Schizophrenias*. "The underlying expectation is that a student must be mentally healthy to the degree the administration would like [to attend college]. That is saying, essentially, that students should not have a severe mental illness."

Some mental illnesses are related to family history and genetics, trauma, or substance abuse. Studies have also shown that brain abnormalities, such as a decreased volume in the tissue that processes information, may contribute to some mental illnesses. The good news is that when mental health issues are identified early and people get help, they are more likely to live fulfilling lives. Therapy and medications can help control many of the debilitating symptoms of mental illnesses. But frequently people— especially young people—don't get the help they need. This is often due to the stigma surrounding mental illness.

## GETTING BETTER: MENTAL HEALTH DAYS FOR STUDENTS

"High school can be a lonely, difficult place to begin with," said Hailey Hardcastle. When Hailey was a senior in Oregon, she spent months lobbying for student mental health days. She explained, "There's so much more pressure these days—getting into college, the social pressure, even just the state of the world and what you're exposed to with climate change, and everything going on with politics. A lot of times it can feel like the world is about to end." The ability to take a mental health day can help when you are overwhelmed by all this pressure.

Because of the rising rates of anxiety, depression, and suicide among young people, some public schools are allowing students to take mental health days as excused absences. This includes schools in Arizona, Colorado, Connecticut, Illinois, Maine, Nevada, Oregon, Utah, and Virginia. Other states are likely to implement similar policies.

# THE STIGMA OF MENTAL ILLNESS

About one in twenty-five Americans lives with a serious mental illness such as severe depression, bipolar disorder, or schizophrenia. And according to NAMI, about half of young people between the ages of six and seventeen have a mental health condition. Yet the stigma that mental illness carries means that many people delay seeking treatment. Because of stigma, people may believe stereotypes they hear about mental illness that aren't true. For example, someone may believe that people with a mental illness are dangerous or unlikely to improve with treatment. Some people may have good intentions but feel uncomfortable when they find out that someone they know has a mental health condition. This may make them treat the person— and even the person's family—differently. Mental health stigma can arise when people

- don't understand mental health conditions or have negative biases about them,
- don't know that mental health conditions are illnesses that can be treated successfully,
- think that a person's mental health condition is "their own fault" or that they can "just get over it," or
- are afraid they might someday have a mental illness themselves.

Unfortunately, people experiencing stigma may feel shame or guilt about having a mental illness. They may not want other people to know about their condition because they fear their family and friends will treat them poorly or even avoid them. This self-stigma may prevent people from seeking treatment. It can keep them from working toward their personal goals—such as going to college or finding a job—even though having a mental health condition is nothing to be ashamed of. And the risk of facing prejudice and discrimination in social and professional circles creates a huge barrier to talking about or seeking help for mental illnesses. For example, some jobs require their potential employees to submit to a drug test before they are hired. These tests may identify a prescription medication for a mental health condition. When the employer discovers the medication, they may choose not to hire that person because the employer may believe that they would not be as successful in the job as someone without a mental health disorder.

Amanda Lipp says, "The stigma of mental illness can greatly affect people's lives. We can't control how other people feel, but we can control what we feel. Walk the walk. Talk the talk. Stand strong. Stigma will never disappear, but we can view ourselves in a better way. Don't allow the stigma of mental illness to keep you from getting the help you need. Don't allow others to stigmatize you, and don't do it to yourself."

## BARRIERS TO CARE

Stigma prevents about 40 percent of people with anxiety and depression from seeking the help they need. Other factors also make it challenging to get care. In the United States, mental health care may be too expensive for many people to afford. While most insurance companies provide some coverage for mental health, copayments—the amount the patient must pay for doctors' appointments and medications—can be high. Insurance benefits may be limited to just a few visits to a therapist. Or in some cases, patients have no health insurance.

And there is a chronic shortage of medical providers in the United States, especially of mental health–care

After the onset of the COVID-19 pandemic, the number of people reporting mental health concerns such as anxiety or depression increased. Unfortunately, there are not enough mental health professionals to support the increase in patients. Many current mental health–care professionals are nearing retirement, meaning we need even more new providers to meet mental health needs.

professionals. Up to one-fourth of Americans may experience a mental health problem or misuse alcohol or drugs during their lifetime. All of these people may need treatment, yet we are far short of the needed mental health professionals. By one estimate, we will need an additional fifteen thousand providers by 2025 to address mental health conditions and addiction. Rural areas may have only a few—or no—mental health providers. In urban areas, mental health providers often have long waiting lists, and patients can't get into their first appointment for months. And insurance companies may not pay mental health providers adequately. Then fewer hospitals and clinics choose to offer those services. Some mental health providers only accept new patients who can cover the full price for treatment themselves.

## THE RIPPLE EFFECT OF MENTAL ILLNESS

Mental illness affects lives in many ways. NAMI says:

- People with a serious mental illness have an increased risk for diseases such as diabetes, cancer, and heart conditions.
- Nearly one in five people with a mental health condition also has a substance use disorder.
- One in five [unhoused] people has a mental illness.
- More than one-third of incarcerated people also have a mental health condition.
- Seven out of ten people in the juvenile justice system have a mental illness.
- Mental health issues and substance abuse cause one-eighth of emergency room visits.

Another factor contributing to inadequate mental health care is the lack of knowledge about mental health and mental illness. What if someone doesn't feel well, but nothing shows up on lab tests or X-rays? Are the symptoms real or imaginary? Even serious mental health conditions may not be obvious to the person with them or to those around them if they don't share their thoughts and feelings. People may assume their emotional or mental status is normal and not realize they are experiencing a serious mental illness.

Race also matters when receiving mental health care. One study found that white people are the only group in which the majority of people with serious mental health concerns who want treatment receive it. In the US, Indigenous people experience 2.5 times more psychological distress in a month than the rest of the population. More than half of the people with severe mental illness who are Black, Latinx, or Asian do not get treatment. Jeanne Miranda, a professor of psychiatry at the University of California, Los Angeles, says, "Minorities are often more

## CUTTING HAIR, CUTTING STIGMA

"The barbershop is the Black man's country club," Trey Cato says. "It's where we can talk without being judged." Cato owns the 2k Tight barbershop in Fort Wayne, Indiana. His shop is part of a movement that seeks to reduce stigma associated with mental health conditions among Black men—a stigma that is all too high in that population. "My shop is a safe haven," Cato says. "I try to build relationships; I try to speak life."

Cato is part of the Confess Project, an organization that helps Black barbers talk to their clients about mental health concerns. The organization pairs participants with mental health professionals in a yearlong training program. Graduates of the program are certified mental health advocates who bridge the gap between the Black community and traditional health-care providers. Black people may be wary of traditional medical systems, which have historically treated them poorly. Obtaining mental health care has even more barriers.

James Garrett Jr., who directs the Indiana Black Barbershop Health Initiative, says, "When our patrons sit in that barber chair, [we] hear many things that are going on in their life. We've got the barbers to engage the patrons, asking, 'How have you been feeling? Have you been sleeping well? Have you been depressed?'" Experts say efforts such as these to remove the stigma of talking about mental health are encouraging.

likely to be poor, less likely to be treated by doctors of their same race and, in many cases, less likely to know they have a condition that requires professional care." Education and support of everyone with mental health conditions should be a priority.

## COPING WITH MENTAL ILLNESS

One in twenty-five Americans lives with a serious mental health condition including anxiety, depression, bipolar disorder, and obsessive-compulsive disorder. Know the signs of mental illness so you can identify them if they show up in a friend or family member. Help that person get the care and support they need and realize they may be reluctant to do so. And avoid contributing to the stigma that mental illness often carries. Do your part to eliminate that stigma. Realize that the condition is not the person's

Amanda Lipp (*left*) was one of several advocates to speak at a panel at the international Together Against Stigma conference in 2015, one of several major events at which participants work to destigmatize mental illness.

fault and that symptoms can usually improve with treatment. That's what happened with Amanda Lipp.

Lipp has changed her life since she had a mental health breakdown in college. She's now a public speaker and documentary filmmaker. Lipp has given over 150 talks at schools and organizations across the United States, sharing her story and films. She's also a research associate at the Center for Applied Research Solutions, a national center that specializes in mental health, behavioral health, and LGBTQIA+ issues. Lipp's The Giving Gallery is an online art sales site to raise funds for mental health organizations and diverse artists. Her work in mental health has been featured in magazines and newspapers and has earned her awards. She's at a good place in her life and says, "Now I feel that I am strong, smart, and beautiful, and that society accepts me for who I am."

If you or a loved one are experiencing a mental health crisis, call 988 or (800) 273-8255 to be connected to the Suicide and Crisis Lifeline.

# CHAPTER 3

# I'M MORE THAN A JUNKIE: LIVING WITH THE STIGMA OF ADDICTION

It was a perfect Mother's Day for Donna Kull of Hillsborough, New Jersey. "The four of us had dinner together on the deck: my husband Brian, our son Adam, and his older sister," Donna says. "It was so pleasant—just what every mother hopes for— her grown children together and seemingly happy, everyone enjoying just being together for a meal."

Three days later, Donna was at her desk in the office where she worked as secretary for a group of high school guidance counselors. "The call that changed our family's life forever came at 7:45 a.m.," Donna recalls. The mother of one of Adam's friends was on the phone. "She was nervous, even a bit hysterical. It seemed like I had to pull the words out of her. 'Donna, these kids,' she said. 'I just don't know. He's gone.'

'Who?' I screamed. 'Who's gone?' 'Adam,' she said. 'He's dead at his apartment.' I yelled, 'NO! No, not Adam!"'

Donna's coworkers heard her anguished cry and gathered around her. "I said that my son had died, and I needed to go. They wanted to take me, told me that I shouldn't drive, but I wouldn't listen. I don't remember my thoughts; I just knew that I had to leave and get to where Adam was. I grabbed my things and cursed God as I ran for my car. I drove as quickly as I could to Adam's apartment." Donna knew Adam used heroin, and she suspected an overdose had killed him.

She was right.

## ADDICTION IN AMERICA

Stories similar to Adam's are far too common in the United States. Drug overdoses and deaths can happen anywhere: in large cities; in small towns, rural areas, and suburbs; in both poor and wealthy neighborhoods; and in small apartments and large homes. Who dies of drug overdoses? A teenaged athlete taking Vicodin for a football injury. A woman in college taking Percocet for a broken ankle and Valium for anxiety. A farmworker who was injured on the job taking the prescription medication OxyContin. An unemployed coal miner using heroin because it's cheaper than the prescribed painkillers he took for his back pain.

Celebrities who started out taking prescription painkillers, became addicted, and eventually died from overdoses include musicians Prince and Michael Jackson and professional wrestler Chyna. Others, such as singer Amy Winehouse, died of alcohol poisoning, and actor and musician River Phoenix died from an overdose of cocaine and heroin. Overdose victims include teens and twentysomethings with bright futures, high school and college athletes, blue- and white-collar workers, parents with young children, older adults living with chronic pain, and people of every race and ethnicity.

Unintentional injuries (including drug overdoses, auto accidents, and falls) are by far the leading cause of death in the United States. About 72,000 people died of accidental drug overdoses in 2019. That number rose dramatically during the COVID-19 pandemic. From April 2020 to April 2021, drug overdose deaths surged to about 100,300. Drug overdose deaths from alcohol, opioids (including heroin, oxycodone, hydrocodone, and fentanyl), methamphetamine, cocaine, and prescription medications have tripled in the past thirty years.

Prince had been taking prescribed painkillers for several years before his overdose in April 2016. Health officials believe he accidentally overdosed on fentanyl when he took a counterfeit Vicodin pill.

For some people the initial decision to try alcohol or illegal drugs may be a choice. According to the National Institute on Drug Abuse (NIDA) people begin taking drugs or alcohol for several reasons:

- *To feel good*. Drugs can produce feelings of pleasure, relaxation, and satisfaction.
- *To feel better*. Some people who suffer from stress or depression start using drugs to become less anxious or to decrease depression.
- *To perform better*. Some people want to improve their performance in school, at work, or in sports.
- *Curiosity and peer pressure*. Teens may try alcohol and drugs because they are curious about the effects or because they feel pressured to do so.

For some people, the need to continue to use drugs becomes a serious problem. No single factor can predict if a person will become addicted to drugs. But the more risk factors a person has, the greater the chance that using drugs or alcohol will lead to an addiction. And some factors

Not all peer pressure carries the same weight. Research shows that people are more likely to try alcohol after being pressured by a group of close friends rather than a larger group—such as a party—of strangers.

create a higher risk than others. A person's genes count for about half of that person's risk for addiction. Their environment—including the influence of family and friends who consume alcohol or use drugs—also contributes to the risk of addiction. Genetic and environmental factors interact with developmental stages in a person's life. During adolescence, areas in the brain that control decision-making, judgment, and self-control are not yet fully developed, so teens are more prone to risky behaviors, such as trying drugs and alcohol, than adults are. And the earlier that drug use begins, the more likely it may progress to addiction.

According to NIDA, "The initial decision to take drugs is typically voluntary. But with continued use, a person's ability to exert self-control can become seriously impaired. This impairment in self-control is the hallmark of addiction." Drugs and alcohol affect the brain, *changing* the way it works, specifically in the area that controls judgment, decision-making, learning, memory, and behavior. This makes addiction a medical condition, and it should be treated as such. The likelihood of developing an addiction varies from person to person and from drug to drug. Cravings or strong desires to use a drug may lead to addiction. NIDA says factors that decrease the risk for addiction include the ability to maintain self-control, parental support, positive relationships, good grades, and antidrug policies. To "just stop" drinking alcohol or taking a drug that has changed the way the brain works is extremely difficult. NIDA says:

As with most other chronic diseases, such as diabetes, asthma, or heart disease, treatment for drug addiction generally isn't a cure. But addiction is treatable and can be successfully managed. People who are recovering from an addiction will be at risk for relapse for years and possibly for their whole lives. Research shows that combining addiction treatment medicines with behavioral therapy ensures the best chance of success for most patients. Treatment approaches tailored to each patient's drug use patterns and any co-occurring medical, mental, and social problems can lead to continued recovery.

That's good news. But the bad news is that only one-tenth of the nearly twenty-one million Americans who are addicted to alcohol or drugs receive any treatment. Often people fight their addiction for years before kicking it for good.

## THE STIGMA OF ADDICTION

Illegal drug use is the most stigmatized health condition in the world, according to the Recovery Research Institute associated with Harvard Medical School. In a study designed to reveal the stigma of substance abuse, researchers asked participants how they felt about two people who were using drugs and alcohol. The study identified one person as a "substance abuser" and the other as having a "substance abuse disorder." When asked about the "substance abuser" the participants' answers clearly showed they held negative stereotypes about people who experience addiction. Compared to the person with a "disorder," the "abuser" was thought to be less likely to benefit from treatment, more likely to benefit from punishment, more likely to be a threat to society, and more able to get over their addiction if they tried. The American Psychological Association finds that people with addictions are often seen as criminals, poor employees, and people who lack a moral compass.

## ALISHA'S STORY

Alisha Choquette had everything going for her during the first year of high school in Stonington, Connecticut. She was a cheerleader, dated the high school quarterback, and partied on the weekends with her friends, all while keeping her grades up. Then a close family friend died. "I was extremely anxious about having to attend the wake," Alisha says. "One of my friends handed me two pills and said they'd help me get through it. This was the day I met and fell in love with the love of my life—opioids."

She recalls: "I remember the feeling I got from taking these pills. They made me feel as if nothing else in the entire world mattered, and all I wanted to focus on was chasing that initial warm rush. All the anxiety associated with life's problems was gone. It was as if I'd morphed into an entirely new person. It was a feeling I wanted to have for the rest of my life—a feeling I would go to any lengths to chase."

Alisha continued to use drugs during high school. "By the end of my senior year, I'd hide behind my textbook in order to feed my pill addiction without being noticed." Things got worse after she graduated. "I was finding ways to get more drugs, so I decided college would have to wait. Since my family was well off, it was easy for me to get by. My mother would send me to the bank with her debit card to get cash for her. Then I'd use the card to dispense more money for me. I gave her the first receipt, but she never knew about the money I took for me. I did this for years. Despite the guilt I felt for stealing from my own mother, the addiction was too powerful for me to stop." Once Choquette's aunt was in a bad auto accident, and Choquette stole her painkillers. "She had her OxyContin in a lockbox, and I picked the lockbox and stole the medication to feed my habit. I wasn't concerned with what she would do when she needed her painkillers, and they were gone."

Choquette got pregnant when she was twenty years old.

**I kept telling myself I was going to stop taking drugs, but the addiction was just too powerful. I would lay awake at night rubbing my belly and promising the baby that I would do better. The next morning, I'd wake up with every intention of not taking drugs, but the craving would take over and I'd give in to temptation. I loved my unborn child more than anything in this entire world, except for opioids. I promised myself that once my baby came into this world, I was going to change my life around. Instead, my addiction just grew stronger.**

After the baby was born, child protective services—an agency that tries to protect children from living in an unsafe environment—placed Choquette's daughter with relatives because she was not capable of caring for the baby.

Over the next few years, Choquette turned to heroin because it was cheaper than the illegal opioid pills she'd been taking. She was arrested, then released to a drug diversion program, which she failed. After receiving four tickets for DUIs (driving under the influence) in one month, a judge sent Choquette to prison for a year. Meanwhile, her mother died. Choquette spent most of that prison term reflecting on her life. When she was released, she was determined to turn her life around permanently.

"Being a drug addict is a lifelong commitment that I would not wish on anybody," Choquette says. "Addiction does not discriminate. It doesn't care where you come from, what you look like, who you know, or what kind of person you are. Anyone can become addicted and once they are, they become someone they never would have believed they were capable of becoming.

"I have faced a lot of stigma associated with being an addict. When people find out you're an addict, they automatically portray you as a dirty, degrading, heartless, indecent human being. You go to your family's house for a holiday, and they hide their pocketbooks because they think that you're going to steal from them." Choquette points out that people don't view addiction as a disease and don't realize that it's a medical condition:

A diabetic can take medication and it's accepted by society. And when you go to a funeral for someone who died of a heart attack, it's sad. But when you read an obituary about somebody who died from a heroin overdose, the reaction is very different. It's like "another addict died and it's no big deal." People are dying every day from the disease of addiction, but it's not being taken as seriously as it should be. There's no pill to take for addiction. There's no cure. Instead, it's a fight that you must fight every day for the rest of your life.

Many people may read my story and be disgusted by the fact that I used drugs while pregnant and "chose" drugs over my child. The truth of the matter is, I love my daughter more than anything in this entire world. I've been clean since December of 2018. Some people say that relapse is a part of recovery. Not everyone has relapses during their recovery, but it is a part of my story. Unfortunately, I couldn't get it right the first few times, but I learn something new with each relapse.

Many people experiencing addiction want to stop drinking or taking illegal drugs. What keeps them from getting the help they need? It could be lack of insurance or limited coverage for addiction treatment. It could be that too few providers offer care for addiction. Sometimes, when a person with an addiction does seek care, the stigma of addiction prevents assistance. For example, providers may believe the stereotype that the addiction is the patient's fault. Their prejudice may lead to discrimination, and the provider may decline to see the patient. Or the stigma of addiction may lead doctors to doubt that someone with an addiction is facing a medical emergency when the person goes to the emergency room. Instead, they may assume that the person is looking to get more drugs. People with addictions often internalize this stigma. They feel ashamed and may refuse to seek treatment.

Often the stigma of being addicted to drugs or alcohol is overwhelming, making it much more difficult to recover. Family members, friends, and the general public may use words such as "junkie," "alcoholic," or "crackhead" to describe a person with an addiction. The stigma of addiction leads to poor self-esteem and worsening mental health. It also contributes to higher rates of crime against people with addictions and sometimes to law enforcement officers feeling less urgency in solving those crimes.

Nora D. Volkow works with the National Institutes of Health and blogged about the stigma of addiction. She believes people need to recognize that environment and genetics influence addiction. She wrote, "Medical care is often necessary to facilitate recovery as well as avert the worst outcomes, like overdose. When people with addiction are stigmatized and rejected, especially by those within healthcare, it only contributes to the vicious cycle that entrenches their disease."

The Kulls, who lost their son Adam to an overdose of heroin and fentanyl, talked about another kind of stigma that most people don't realize exists. "There's a stigma we faced as parents who've lost a child to an overdose," Brian Kull explained. "After Adam's death, our social circle was reduced by about half. This was partially our choosing. We decided to shed relationships that lacked compassion and caring. But part of this was thrust upon us due to the stigma of his death. We quickly realized some people were uncomfortable with the details and made an effort to avoid us in public. Eventually these friendships ended."

## ADDICTION ESSENTIALS

Overdose deaths from illegal drugs, prescription drugs, and alcohol have tripled in the past thirty years. Often people decide to try illegal drugs or alcohol. But drugs and alcohol can alter brain chemistry so that it affects judgment, decision-making, and behavior. These changes turn addiction into a medical problem, not just one of choosing to use these substances. Of course, not everyone who takes illegal (or legal) drugs or alcohol becomes addicted. Factors such as a person's genetic makeup, the environment they live in, and a person's own level of self-control help keep addiction from developing. Addiction cannot be cured, but it can be managed with the proper treatment. That's why people with addictions generally say they are in recovery. And that recovery is a lifelong process.

After completing community college, Choquette became a licensed chemical dependency professional. She's an advanced substance use disorder clinician doing psychiatric telehealth in New England. This job puts her insight and experience in dealing with addiction to good use. She also shares her story through an organization called Shine a Light on Heroin. Its goal is to reduce the stigma of heroin addiction. Choquette says, "I believe we can either use our experiences as a means to get down on ourselves and live with shame and regret, or we can use our experiences as a platform to reach better things in our life. I have chosen to use my negative experiences, to learn from them, and to use them to help others who are afflicted by this terrible disease of addiction. I'm finally comfortable in my own skin and am okay with the woman that I've become."

# CHAPTER 4

# UNHOUSED: DON'T JUDGE ME BY WHERE I LIVE

Can you imagine having nowhere to call home? Or owning little more than a sleeping bag and camping out on a public sidewalk or in the doorway of a shop that's closed for the night? How about living in an old car or an abandoned building? Or having all your possessions in a shopping cart you "borrowed" from a grocery store parking lot? Chances are you've met or gone to school with someone in situations like these, and you didn't even know it.

An estimated 580,000 people in the United States are unhoused. That number could be significantly higher because it's difficult to accurately count a population that frequently moves around and often tries to avoid being seen. Los Angeles and New York City have the highest number of unhoused people in the United States. About two-thirds of that population are single people, while the remainder are teens who have left home or families with children.

## WHAT DOES *HOMELESS* MEAN?

*Homeless* is a term rapidly dropping out of use. The organization Unhoused.org says, "The label of 'homeless' has derogatory connotations. It implies that one is 'less than', and it undermines self-esteem. The use of the term *unhoused* instead has a profound personal impact upon those with insecure housing situations. It implies that there is a moral and social assumption that everyone should be housed in the first place."

Eve Garrow works for the American Civil Liberties Union and advocates for the unhoused. "We've seen this before, words like *transient* or *hobo* are retired and no longer acceptable to use. *Homeless* has become intertwined with narratives that are toxic. It deserves to be retired." Yet the word *homeless* is still widely used by the public and the media.

People are considered unhoused if they don't have a permanent place to live such as a house, apartment, or condo. They may be living in tents or under blankets in public places such as parks, streets, or doorways. Some sleep in temporary or emergency shelters. Some live in their cars or vans and move to different locations each day. Others "couch surf" from one friend or relative's house to another because they don't have a house or apartment of their own.

Sister Libby Fernandez, a nun who spent twenty years working at Sacramento's Loaves & Fishes, said in a magazine article, "[The number of unhoused people] has jumped almost 50 percent from two years ago [and] . . . all the shelters are full. There's a waiting list just to get into an emergency shelter. There are [yearslong] waiting lists for

# JOE'S STORY

Joseph David Smith says he grew up in a poor family where drug use and prison time were common. "One day I kind of hit a wall where life was getting to be too much for me, and the job I had was closing in." Smith explains:

> I walked away from everything. I was homeless for more than five years. Part of the time, I lived in a tent along the American River Parkway in Sacramento. Then I moved to another part of town with some other folks I knew who were camping. I got some temporary work as a day laborer, but that dried up. I bounced around between Sacramento and San Francisco, where I had lived as a teen, and camped in Golden Gate Park. Then, I spent time in Reno with a friend I'd camped with, but all roads kept leading back to Sacramento. That's where I spent most of my homeless years.

Smith says he was an alcoholic in those days:

> I was an unsightly drunk, the guy you walked around, the guy you stayed away from because I was sloppy and dirty. Things weren't looking so good for sure. During the last several years of living outside, the alcoholism got pretty bad, and I started to suffer physically. If I didn't drink, I'd have withdrawal symptoms and needed to be hospitalized. There was a center run by Volunteers of America (VOA) where I went to sober up. Every time I couldn't get enough alcohol, I went to the center to withdraw, and each time was worse than the time before.

As if being unhoused and having an addiction to alcohol weren't enough, Smith discovered he also had hepatitis C, a virus that attacks the liver. He recalls, "And there I am, drinking like a madman on top of hepatitis C, even knowing that alcohol is very bad for the liver. I went into the VOA center to withdraw for the final time in April, 2011. When I woke up a few days later, I was as yellow as could be, which is a sign of severe liver damage." The staff at the VOA center made an appointment for Joe to see a doctor who told him that the hepatitis would probably kill him if he didn't stop drinking.

"Alcoholism is a powerful thing," Smith says.

**I never drank again after that, but the first few weeks were horrible. I was very sick, and all I could think about was wanting to drink. The folks at the shelter put me in contact with Alcoholics Anonymous [AA] who started to work with me. I got a sponsor to help me stay sober. The shelter let me stay, knowing that if I had to leave, I was going to go out and drink. Detox is hell wrapped up in hell. The meds they give you help, but it's still awful. I've been sober since April 2011, and AA has been my rock.**

People at the VOA shelter helped Smith apply for disability assistance because he was still too sick to work. "After I'd been sober for six months, I got a little room in a house that I could afford with the disability payments. I've been off the streets since then. I ran into some friends living the sober life and began to hang around with them. I left the room in the house and moved into a more stable environment."

Four years after Smith went to the VOA, his doctor wanted him to get up and "shake the cobwebs" off. In 2016 he started volunteering at Loaves & Fishes, in Sacramento, California, an organization that helps the unhoused. After working as a volunteer for several months, Loaves & Fishes hired Smith.

"There's a lot of stigma when you're homeless," Smith says and adds:

> A lot of the angry stuff I heard came from people walking or driving by me. "We're tired of seeing you homeless people in our neighborhood." "Go find somewhere else to be." "Get a job. Get a life!" And "Sober up, why don't you?" But people living outside are people just like anyone else. They have stories, and they've lived lives. Remember that most people on the street are not unhoused through any fault of their own. Something went horribly wrong with their lives. Maybe they lost a job, had health problems, or were evicted from their home because they couldn't afford the rent. Once you've been on the street, you're stuck. Making your way out of that is tough.

Often people who are unhoused are mistreated and alone. Smith says a simple act of kindness can help: "You can engage with them. The public has painted homeless people as people who are less than human. It becomes very easy when you look at people through that lens to treat them badly. Most people living outside are not addicts and they're not criminals. Homelessness is a condition someone is forced to live in. It's not the person."

affordable housing. There are even waiting lists to get into recovery or emergency beds. That is a very serious issue."

## NO PLACE TO GO

Far more single men than single women are unhoused. Other unhoused people include families with small children and young people who have left their parents' home for safety or other reasons. About 23 percent of unhoused people in America are Latinx, and 39 percent are Black, even though

Black people make up only 13 percent of the population.

The reasons for the hundreds of thousands of unhoused people in the United States include these:

- **Lack of affordable housing.**
  The US Department of Housing and Urban Development defines affordable housing as "housing on which the occupant is paying no more than 30 percent of gross income for housing costs, including utilities." Yet many people cannot find housing that fits into that definition. Housing prices are often much higher than people can afford with 30 percent of their wages. For example, a person must earn $39 per hour to afford to rent a two-bedroom house in California, $34 per hour in New York, $25 per hour in Florida, $24 per hour in Virginia, and $22 per hour in Texas. Factors that contribute to the housing-salary disparity include insufficient state and federal funding for building and maintaining housing that people can afford. Foreclosures—the eviction of people who cannot pay their rent or mortgage—increased during the COVID-19 pandemic, forcing more and more people to lose their housing as they lost their jobs.
- **Poverty.**
  Being unhoused and poverty are closely linked. Poor people are frequently unable to pay for housing, food, childcare, utilities, and health care. They must make difficult choices when limited resources can't cover all those necessary expenses. A poor person or a family living in poverty may be just one illness, one accident, or one paycheck away from losing their home.

One solution for the unhoused crisis is to build or maintain rent-controlled or affordable housing. This apartment building opened in Denver, Colorado, in May 2022. Rent prices are based on the median income of jobs such as teachers and first responders who live in the area—people who may require assistance to afford housing.

- *Lack of jobs that pay a living wage.*
  A living wage means that a person or family has enough income to afford shelter, food, health care, and other essential needs. But a state's minimum wage, or the lowest hourly rate a company can pay their employees, is not always high enough to pay for housing. For example, the minimum wage in Texas, Alabama, and several other states is only $7.25 per hour. In contrast, Florida's minimum wage is $11.00 per hour, and California's is $15.00 per hour. While these rates look better, the average cost of living in these states is higher.

Compare the salary from a full-time job (2,080 hours per year) at those hourly rates with the cost of living in these states. Even people with full-time jobs may have such a low income they are unable to find housing they can afford.

| STATE | ANNUAL SALARY AT MINIMUM WAGE ($) | AVERAGE COST OF LIVING ($) |
|---|---|---|
| Texas | 15,080 | 39,661 |
| Virginia | 22,800 | 42,757 |
| Florida | 22,800 | 43,615 |
| California | 31,200 | 46,636 |

- *Lack of affordable health care.*
  Not all jobs provide health insurance to their employees, which can be very expensive to purchase. If someone has no health insurance, unexpected medical bills may make the difference between having a home or not. If someone experiences a severe and persistent mental illness or has a substance use disorder, and cannot afford treatment, these conditions can worsen their struggle with expenses, holding a job, or affording a home.
- *Abusive relationship.*
  Survivors of intimate partner violence must sometimes choose between remaining in an abusive relationship or leaving the abuser and their only option for a home.

- *Mental illness.*
  According to *Psychology Today*, an estimated 20 to 25 percent of the US unhoused population suffers from severe mental illness, compared to 6 percent of the general public. This makes it extremely difficult or impossible for those people to find and remain in a home.
- *Addiction.*
  People with an addiction may struggle to hold down a job. Sometimes they have mental health issues and live in poverty. These factors greatly increase the risk for losing a house or apartment.

## THE STIGMA OF BEING UNHOUSED

In a study cited in *Psychology Today*, researchers collected 1 percent of all Twitter posts containing the word *homeless*. Researchers examined a random sample of the 1.75 million tweets to learn more about the stigma faced by unhoused people. The study showed that many people believe stereotypes and hold prejudices against the unhoused that included these:

- *"Homeless people are dirty."*
  There is a widespread lack of public bathrooms in the United States, and stores often refuse to allow the unhoused to use facilities reserved for customers. The tweets often referred to unhoused people as somehow less than human because they failed to keep clean.
- *"Homeless people are socially deviant."*
  This was especially used to refer to unhoused people asking for help. People often viewed them as scam artists who were faking being unhoused

or begging for money that they would use on drugs or alcohol instead of food. One tweet said, "When I see a homeless person I honestly don't know if they're faking or not, so they gets nothin from me." This attitude can lead to laws banning "panhandlers" or arrests of unhoused people as public nuisances.

- **"Homeless people are threatening, violent, and/or engage in criminal behavior."**
Many of the negative tweets about the unhoused share stories about their "aggressive panhandling" and their sometimes bizarre behavior, which "normal people" find threatening. Yet, unhoused people are far more likely to be victims of crime rather than criminals. For example, one study showed that nearly half of unhoused people experienced violence, including harassment and violent injury (often from police), compared to just 2 percent of the general population.

- **"Homeless people deserve to be homeless."**
Many of the tweets focused on the problems that unhoused people might have, suggesting their unhoused situation was the result of substance abuse, mental illness, or their own bad behavior.

- **"People are homeless because they are lazy."**
Many of the tweets condemning the unhoused say they have character flaws. One tweet stated, "Yes I drink and smoke sometimes, but I'm not going to end up homeless, I have goals and I'm going to accomplish them." Another claimed, "I only give homeless people money if they are old or disabled."

Attitudes like these make the lives of unhoused people more difficult and dangerous than they already are. Another stereotype of unhoused people is that they are unreliable. Some employers who believe this stereotype won't allow people to apply for jobs without a home address. This is a form of discrimination against unhoused people. When they cannot find a job, how can people make enough money to pay for housing to change their situation? And without a job, unhoused people appear to fit the stereotype that they are not trying to get out of poverty.

Sister Libby understands this stigma and its results all too well. "The biggest thing about the stigma of homelessness is that people don't treat the unhoused like human beings," she says. "People lump them into the category of 'homeless' so they must be mentally ill and use drugs. People don't want to look at the homeless as individuals, who they are, their experience, and education. But each of us has a unique story. To break stigma, you've got to see the unhoused as individuals, to know them by name and get to know who they are. Also, let them know who you are, so it becomes an equal relationship. It's all about giving and getting respect."

## AN EDUCATOR'S ANSWER

A few years ago, Maralyn Soifer was assistant principal at an elementary school near a shelter in the Los Angeles area. The school taught many unhoused students who were temporarily living in the shelter. School staff took steps to prevent those children from being stigmatized by their classmates. "In most cases, students knew when a child was from a shelter or living in temporary housing," she says. "The school also knew which children were unhoused because parents have to identify where they live before a child can get into a new school. However, being unhoused didn't prevent them from registering their children. It was also easy to recognize these children because their clothing usually didn't fit properly. They also came to school early to get breakfast."

Soifer felt fortunate to be in a school where students had sensitive parents and teachers, so the unhoused children felt no stigma. She recalls, "Teachers would assign a buddy to any new student who arrived at the school whether they were unhoused or not. The buddy helped the new student adjust to the school by becoming a friend and introducing the newcomer to other students. Being a buddy was considered an honor for the students, and they enjoyed helping out a new friend. School supplies were available to all new students, so there was no stigma to not having pencils and other supplies."

Soifer believes the most difficult part of keeping unhoused students in school was that they were so transient. "We often lost them to another shelter, or they just disappeared. One child really wanted to stay at our school. His parents found a place to live that wasn't in our district. That little ten-year-old took three buses from where his new home was just so he could come back and finish his year at our school."

Soifer has some advice about how kids of various ages can work to prevent the stigma of being unhoused in themselves and others. She says, "Elementary-aged children can volunteer with their parents at organizations such as food banks. Kids can open a simple lemonade stand and donate the proceeds to organizations that help the homeless. As students enter middle school and high school, they can do more. For example, many colleges expect applicants to have performed community service. This can include tutoring students at Boys and Girls Clubs, or assisting teachers in a Head Start program, or even running a food drive at school."

# SUCCESS STORY: JOSHUA MORRONE'S ART

Joshua Morrone of San Jose, California, experienced mental illness and was unhoused for several years. He now takes medication every day to manage his mental health and lives in an independent living facility. Morrone photographs the world he sees around him in his own unique way. While Morrone is not a professional photographer, his work is striking.

*And Still They Won't Stop* was captured by Morrone after a car killed a friend at this intersection.

Morrone took *Afternoon under a Bridge* after he dreamed about a bridge.

This is an image of a taqueria Morrone likes. Note the tray of food against the café's curtains. He calls it *Reflections of Burritos*.

Stigma can be greatly reduced when young people see that adults and peers respect those who might otherwise have been stigmatized.

## HOUSING THE UNHOUSED

More than half a million Americans have no permanent home. And the problems that cause people to become unhoused probably won't disappear soon. These include a lack of affordable housing, a lack of jobs that pay a living wage, and a lack of affordable health care—these also contribute to poverty. Negative and inaccurate beliefs about the unhoused make it even more difficult for them to find and maintain housing. In some communities, a county or state may propose building a shelter for the unhoused. Local citizens object, and the project is canceled or put on hold, usually due to stigma, prejudice, and discrimination against the unhoused. We can do more for that population. Funding to decrease homelessness is needed, as is better education of the public.

After Joe Smith had volunteered at Loaves & Fishes for three months, Sister Libby hired him to be a janitor at the facility. He then worked his way up the ranks. "Now I'm the Advocacy Director at Loaves & Fishes," he says. "I advocate on behalf of guests—the men, women, and children experiencing homelessness. I work with the advocacy community to help people find the housing and other services they need. My primary job is to build relationships with everyone—from the person living outside, to the city hall official, to state and local officials, and everybody in between. So, when a person comes to me needing help, I can help connect them with someone that may be able to help them."

# CHAPTER 5

# RELATIONSHIP VIOLENCE: LIVING WITH FEAR

Victims of intimate partner violence (IPV)—also called domestic violence—do not bring violence upon themselves. It is never their fault. Violence or abuse may occur when one person feels entitled to have power over their partner—whether they are dating or married—and chooses to gain and maintain that control through abuse. Intimate partner violence doesn't always involve physical injury or physical abuse. Abusers can control their partners with intimidation and fear. And IPV can happen to teens and young people who are dating.

# WHAT IS INTIMATE PARTNER VIOLENCE?

Intimate partner violence is the emotional and often physical acts intended to control or harm someone in a close relationship. It can happen in both heterosexual and LGBTQIA+ relationships. IPV can occur in many forms: slapping, hitting, threats, intimidation, isolation, coercion, and blaming. The National Coalition Against Domestic Violence says, "Anyone can be a victim of domestic violence. There is NO 'typical victim.' Victims of domestic violence come from all walks of life, varying age groups, all backgrounds, all communities, all education levels, all economic levels, all cultures, all ethnicities, all religions, all abilities, and all lifestyles."

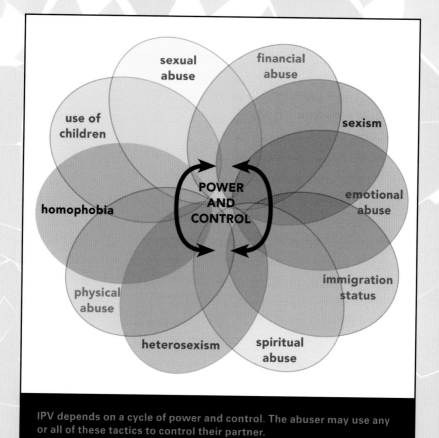

IPV depends on a cycle of power and control. The abuser may use any or all of these tactics to control their partner.

# JILL'S STORY

Jill Summers was only fifteen when she met Lucas at school. "When we first met, I had just moved in with my grandparents," Jill says. "My mother has schizophrenia and was too unstable to take care of me. My grandparents took me in and finished raising me. I was a sophomore starting a new school and I had to leave all my friends behind. I was really depressed.

"Then I met Lucas in my biology class, but I wasn't attracted to him until he wrote me a sweet letter that touched my heart. He wanted to go out but didn't have the courage to ask me. We started dating. He was always very affectionate. We would hold hands, kiss between classes, and he'd walk me home from school. He was my first relationship and my first love."

She was easy to manipulate, a characteristic that abusers often exploit, even if the abuser is the same age. "I had a purity ring, and I wanted to save myself for marriage. Lucas started to beg me for sex. I kept telling him no, that I wasn't going to have sex until I was married. Then he proposed. I was surprised but agreed to marry Lucas because I loved him. He promised me that we'd get married when we were eighteen. I finally gave in to his begging. I never took my purity ring off because I was ashamed and didn't want my family to know that I wasn't a virgin anymore."

Jill and Lucas dated for over a year until he broke up with her without giving her a reason. Instead, their relationship morphed into "friends with benefits." When Jill got tired of that arrangement, she dated someone else, and Lucas got jealous. He wanted her back. For several years, they were off and on again. "Every time I would start to get over him, he would plead with me to come back. He never really wanted me, but he never could let me go. Lucas was mean to me all the time, but I couldn't see it because I desperately wanted to make our relationship work. I couldn't see myself being married to anyone but him."

Jill didn't understand that Lucas wanted to control her. He told her that she couldn't cut her hair. He called her a clown when she wore makeup. He also demanded obedience. He controlled her financially. She couldn't even go to the grocery store alone. Sexual abuse became the norm. She says, "He'd hold me down and do things I didn't like. I felt powerless because he was stronger than me. I was alone with him and there was nothing I could do." After five years, Jill finally left Lucas, but she didn't leave him for good.

Lucas pursued her off and on for a few more years. She returned to him again, even though nothing had changed. But one night she got a call from Lucas's father saying that his son had been arrested. He'd planned to meet a fourteen-year-old girl for sex in a park. Lucas had been talking to the girl online for a month, but she wasn't real—he was actually talking to a female police officer who was pretending to be a young girl. Jill said, "Lucas called me from jail all the time saying he was sorry, and that he loved me, and he'd been stupid. He told me that he had no intention of doing anything with the girl, because he knew she was fake and only went to the park to prove it. But enough was enough, and it was the final straw."

Stigma was part of the reason she stayed with Lucas for so long. She never told her family about the abuse she was enduring because she was too ashamed. "I didn't tell them what was going on behind closed doors, and my low self-esteem made me feel like I wasn't worthy of anyone else's love. After I got away from Lucas, all the memories of how he treated me came back. Even now I question myself and really feel dumb for letting him treat me so badly all those years."

IPV can happen between intimate partners regardless of gender and sexual orientation. While IPV can take many forms, it's always about gaining and maintaining power and control over the victim. According to the Woman Against Abuse organization, intimate partner violence may include behaviors such as

- *Physical abuse.* Hitting, slapping, punching, kicking, or strangling the victim. The abuser may damage personal property, not allow medical care, control medication use, or even use weapons.
- *Emotional abuse.* This abuse includes

## MARIELLE'S STORY

"Marielle" asked that her real name or photo not be used.

When Marielle Roberts started college, she was eager to learn and to have new experiences. She and her friends made bets on who would be first in their group to date. Although Marielle had no particular interest in dating, she was the first of her friends to do so.

"It wasn't love at first sight; I fell gradually but intensely in love," Marielle says. "Early on, he pushed for commitment in ways that made me uncomfortable, but I relegated the small alarm bells to the back of my mind. What did I know? I had never been with anyone before. Denial and love are a potent and often lethal combination."

Several months into the relationship, Marielle's partner raped her. "Someone I loved and who I thought loved me, raped me. Again and again." At first, she believed the rapes "happened to her." But Roberts soon understood what the rapes were. She says, "Calling these rapes 'something that happened' is damaging, as if being assaulted by a partner is simply due to fate. Rape didn't just happen. It was done to me. There are large slices of my memory I will never get back, which perhaps is a blessing. Even now, years name-calling, insulting, blaming, humiliating, or isolating the partner, or controlling what the partner does and where the partner goes.

- *Sexual abuse.* Sexual abuse is more about power than sex. It can include sexual behavior performed without consent, such as forcing a partner to have sex with others, hurting a partner during sex, and demanding sexual activity when the victim is afraid to say no.
- *Technological abuse.* This form of abuse uses technology to control and stalk a partner. It's more common among teens who may use social

later, it's hard to reconcile the person I thought he was with the person I now know he is."

Marielle didn't know anyone who had been assaulted by their romantic partner—the person they loved. She recalls, "When I talked to friends about the abuse, I could tell they wondered why I loved a man who treated me so badly. Not everyone believed me. And some even sided with him. There's real stigma in being assaulted by your intimate partner. It isolated me. I felt I had no support or understanding. If I hadn't faced such stigma about intimate partner sexual violence, I wonder if I would have left earlier, or let go of my self-blame sooner."

Some survivors of assault find healing in forgiveness, but others, such as Marielle, do not. She explains, "While my anger has quieted over the years and slowly retreated into its cave, I will not and cannot forgive him. Any explanation that he could ever offer isn't good enough. I experienced significant healing in the years since I left that relationship. No part of me is still in love with him. Every day, I choose to try to be in love with myself, with the woman who walked away by convincing herself it was the right thing to do. And it was."

media without adult supervision. It includes
hacking into a partner's email and other personal
accounts, using tracking devices in a partner's cell
phone to monitor and control where the partner
goes, and demanding to know passwords to
personal accounts.
- *Financial abuse.* A type of abuse that can include
  taking control of finances, harassing the partner at
  a workplace, harming the partner so the partner
  cannot work, controlling financial assets, or
  putting the partner on an allowance.

Living in a home with intimate partner violence can
profoundly affect children. They may feel guilty about the
abuse they witness, even blaming themselves for it. IPV
can harm child development. It can keep children from
participating in school events, getting good grades, or
forming friendships. Teens who experience intimate partner
violence in their homes might act out in negative ways, such
as fighting with family members or classmates or skipping
school. They may engage in risky behaviors and use alcohol
or drugs. They may bully others and get into trouble with
the police. People who experience IPV have a higher rate of
depression and suicidal thoughts.

More than fifteen million children in the United States
live in homes where IPV has occurred. These children are
at greater risk for repeating the cycle as adults by entering
into abusive relationships or becoming abusers themselves.
For example, a boy who sees his mother being abused is
ten times more likely to abuse his female partner as an
adult. A girl who grows up in a home where her father
abuses her mother is more than six times as likely to be
sexually abused as an adult than a child who grows up in a
nonabusive home.

## ARE YOU A VICTIM OF INTIMATE PARTNER VIOLENCE? DOES YOUR PARTNER . . .

- embarrass or make fun of you in front of your friends or family?
- put down your accomplishments?
- use intimidation or threats to force you to do what they want?
- say that you are nothing without them?
- treat you roughly—grab, push, pinch, shove, or hit you?
- call you frequently or show up to make sure you're where you said you would be?
- use drugs or alcohol as an excuse for saying hurtful things or abusing you?
- blame you for how they feel or act?
- prevent you from doing things you want?
- do or say things to "teach you a lesson"?

If your partner does any of these things to you, you may be experiencing intimate partner violence and abuse. To get help, call the National Domestic Violence Hotline, available 24/7, at (800) 799-7233.

## WHO EXPERIENCES INTIMATE PARTNER VIOLENCE?

According to the Centers for Disease Control and Prevention (CDC), one in four women and one in ten men have reported experiencing IPV. The number could be much higher because many victims and survivors who managed to escape their abusers don't report IPV. These are some statistics:

- Intimate partner violence accounts for 15 percent of all violent crime.
- About 19 percent of IPV involves a weapon, and the presence of a gun increases the risk of murder by five times.
- Women between the ages of eighteen and twenty-four are the group most commonly abused by their intimate partners.
- Only one-third of people injured by intimate partners receive medical care for their injuries.

According to the CDC, about one in twelve American high school students has experienced physical dating violence, sexual dating violence, or both. The risk of partner violence among teens increases if they experienced abuse as children or witnessed violence in their home. Some young people may then believe that violence is a normal part of relationships. Violence in an adolescent relationship sets the stage for problems in future relationships, including intimate partner violence, sexual abuse, and other abuse throughout life.

Teen partner violence isn't recognized as often as it should be. Because most teen victims don't report the abuse, many people aren't aware of how common it is. Half of teens who report dating violence and rape also reported a suicide attempt. This is compared to 12.5 percent of unabused girls and 5.4 percent of unabused boys. Victims are reluctant to tell family and friends, in part because of the stigma associated with it.

## STAYING AND LEAVING

With all the horrors of intimate partner violence, why would any person stay with an abuser? Often in some survivors' minds, the abuser really loves them. Often the abuser has destroyed their partner's self-esteem. One woman who wished to remain anonymous said, "For me, I knew it was my fault. He told me I was a piece of garbage and that I should never have been born. I used to hide in the closet to get away from his horrible words." For some people, the relationship is a mix of hope and love, fear and danger. Should they stay or should they leave? That decision may be difficult for people who haven't been abused to understand. Often victims stay because they worry their abuser may follow through with the threats they've made. For example, the abuser may hurt or kill them or their children, the victim may lose custody of the children, or the abuser may harm or kill pets, friends, or other family members. The abuser may even threaten to kill themself if their partner leaves.

Family and friends may not be aware of the abuse or may not be supportive of a person's need to leave that environment. A victim may not have any money or assets because the abuser has total control over finances. And it can be much harder to leave when children are involved. If they leave their children behind, victims could lose custody and might not be able to get their children back. If the person who was victimized takes their children when they leave, they may become unhoused if they don't have the money to care for multiple people.

Marc L'Ecluse, a marriage and family therapist and certified domestic violence prevention facilitator in California, says, "The fear of being judged can drive us to hide parts of our lives. This can cause us to feel separated from others and ashamed. This shame can lead to a sense of isolation for a victim or survivor of domestic violence. Victims may feel there's no way out. They may believe they are completely dependent on their abuser."

There may be some unexpected hurdles to leaving an abusive relationship. For example, some law enforcement officers treat violence as a "domestic dispute," rather than as a crime of assault. If victims fight back, they are sometimes arrested and charged with assault, even if they are defending themselves against the abuser. Police may discourage the victim from filing charges, may side with the abuser, or may not take the victim's story seriously. And attorneys may be reluctant to prosecute abusers or may convince the abuser to plead guilty to a lesser crime. Judges rarely impose the maximum sentence upon convicted abusers. Probation or fines are much more common. These reactions demonstrate the prevalent stigma of IPV. Historically, IPV has been considered a "normal" part of a relationship and wasn't defined as a crime until the 1970s. Ongoing education about the realities of IPV may help police, attorneys, judges, and all of us to understand the nature of this abuse and how to combat it.

Studies have shown that police inaction, hostility, and disbelief of victims of IPV are some of the top barriers to seeking help from the criminal justice system. Victims of IPV who are part of marginalized communities may be less likely to seek help from law enforcement due to the history of police bias based on gender, race, immigration status, sexuality, and more.

People do manage to escape their abusive environments. But if the abuser suspects the victim is planning to leave, the relationship can become more dangerous. What if it's you or someone you know? Consider finding local resources before leaving or helping someone leave an abusive relationship. States and many cities have organizations with programs to help victims of IPV. The Office on Women's Health's website lists resources in every state. Many of these organizations offer counselors, social workers, and advocates to people suffering intimate partner abuse. Available resources may include emotional support, housing (in a secret facility or a volunteer's home), and legal assistance. The Onslow Women's Center also lists resources for male survivors of intimate partner violence.

When you have the information you need, make plans. Be ready to leave on a moment's notice. If you have access to a car, keep it fueled and facing the street. Hide a spare key if you have one. Try to keep emergency cash, clothing, and important documents stashed at a relative's or friend's house. If you're cut off from other people, find a hiding place in your home for those items. After you leave, protect your privacy so your abuser can't find you. Don't use your cell phone—get a new one. Use a safe computer, one that your abuser doesn't know about. Libraries often have computers available for public use. Change all your passwords. Remember, in this technologically advanced era, it's easy to track people online or by phone use.

It can be dangerous to leave an abusive relationship, but it's more dangerous to stay. As L'Ecluse says, "It requires incredible strength and courage to be able to reach out and ask for help. If you feel you are being abused, reach out to someone you trust, share what is happening to you, and please ask for help."

## INTIMATE PARTNER VIOLENCE IN THE LGBTQIA+ COMMUNITY

Most literature about intimate partner violence is about people in heterosexual relationships. Yet members of the LGBTQIA+ community experience more abuse and violence than do people in heterosexual relationships. Persons of any gender identity and age can be either the perpetrator or the victim. The National Coalition Against Domestic Violence posts these facts about IPV:

- Nearly 44 percent of lesbian and 61 percent of bisexual women have experienced rape, physical violence, stalking by a partner, or a combination of these, as opposed to 35 percent of heterosexual women.
- Twenty-six percent of gay men and 37 percent of bisexual men have experienced rape, physical violence, stalking by a partner, or a combination of these, compared to 29 percent of heterosexual men.
- In a study of male same-sex relationships, only 26 percent called the police for help, even after experiencing near-lethal violence.
- Bisexual people are more likely to experience sexual violence compared to people who don't identify as bisexual.

LGBTQIA+ individuals experience many of the same problems as heterosexual people do when seeking help, but some additional difficulties are unique to this group. For example, abusers may threaten to "out" victims if they are keeping their relationship a secret. While society more readily accepts LGBTQIA+ lifestyles than in the past, some people are not ready for their friends, family, or employers to know. They are not ready to endure the stigma they may face. Health-care providers and their staffs may be homophobic or have little knowledge about IPV in the LGBTQIA+ population. An article in a medical journal about IPV in the LGBTQIA+ community says, "Physicians should learn about legal issues for [LGBTQIA+] individuals and the availability of community or advocacy programs for [LGBTQIA+] perpetrators or victims of IPV."

Resources aimed at heterosexual survivors may not serve all the needs of the LGBTQIA+ community. For example, shelters for survivors of IPV are often for women only, and transgender individuals may not be allowed because of their gender status. But online resources can be a good start to learn more about what's available. Women's Advocates provides a web page about IPV in the LGBTQIA+ community. The Onslow Women's Center also has a website for LGBTQIA+ victims of IPV.

The American Bar Association offers a tool kit designed for legal personnel about LGBTQIA+ individuals that includes many articles, such as an agenda and slides for a presentation, information about workplace discrimination and coming out, and a guide to terminology.

## THE STIGMA OF INTIMATE PARTNER VIOLENCE

As if it isn't bad enough to deal with a violent abuser, survivors often face stigma—stigma if they stay and stigma if they leave. People may say, "You asked for it. Men will be men" or "Women can't abuse men. You're just letting her boss you around." They might ask, "What did you do to make her so angry?" or "If they were abusing you, why didn't you just leave?" These attitudes—suggesting that the victim is at fault—can make it difficult for the survivor to seek help. Survivors of IPV should remember that the abuse is never their fault.

# SURVIVING IPV

Meggie Royer is a survivor of intimate partner violence. After leaving her abusive partner, she recounted her experiences in poems that have been published in multiple journals. She is now a respected advocate for victims of IPV. Royer wrote this poem in 2013. For more of her poems, see https://writingsforwinter.tumblr.com/categories.

## HEART HEAVY AS A FIST

I become an expert at applying concealer
in ten minutes or less;
CoverGirl always knows exactly what shade
will hide black eyes.
Once he slammed me up against the door until the grain
burned across my back like sandpaper;
even now you can still see
the pattern on my spine. My mother asks
where I got the new bracelet.
No, mom, those are bruises that are encircling my wrist.
They cost more than any 50-carat diamond.
And there are always chrysanthemums afterward,
wrapped in foil
just the way I like them, slurred phone calls
in the middle of work
full of stuttering apologies. They always include
the words never again.

Sara Grady, a social worker and director of an anti-stigma group said, "We hear from victims often that they experience feelings of shame, guilt, and responsibility related to being a domestic violence victim. This is why it is so important to widely educate our community that domestic violence is never the victim's fault. Nothing that a victim does warrants them experiencing abuse. Nothing."

Much of the stigma that victims of IPV face is internal. Attorney Wendy Patrick has worked with numerous survivors of intimate partner violence. She says, "Many victims of domestic abuse remain under the radar because they are ashamed that they have chosen to remain in an abusive relationship. Victims are sensitive to the judgment they fear from others. Reporting the perpetrator's behavior would involve revealing embarrassing and humiliating details they would rather never discuss—especially if they have been enduring this treatment for years."

Survivors commonly experience depression, anxiety, post-traumatic stress disorder, and sometimes addiction because of the abuse they suffered. And they may face prejudice and discrimination as part of the stigma of being a survivor of IPV. Once survivors escape their abusers, their family, friends, students, teachers, or employers may treat them differently when details of their abuse become known. People may treat them as if they are fragile or cannot make smart decisions for themselves.

The National Coalition Against Domestic Violence started Domestic Violence Awareness Month to help combat the stigma surrounding partnership violence. During October, staff focuses on educating people about intimate partner violence and spreading awareness of the resources that are available to victims, family and friends of victims, and those who worry that a loved one is in an abusive relationship or experiencing domestic violence.

## OCTOBER IS
# DOMESTIC VIOLENCE
### AWARENESS MONTH

Domestic Violence Awareness Month is represented by a purple ribbon. In the United States, women often wore purple when they were fighting for the right to vote in the early twentieth century. The purple ribbon signifies victims of domestic violence's courage and strength.

## IT'S NEVER YOUR FAULT

Intimate partner violence is never the fault of the victim or survivor. And IPV can happen to anyone whether the person is heterosexual or part of the LBGTQIA+ community. Millions of people have experienced abuse or violence in a close relationship. Witnessing or experiencing IPV profoundly affects children and teens. A child growing up in an abusive household is more likely to become an abuser or to become a victim of IPV as an adult.

The stigma of experiencing intimate partner violence is very real. People may believe that the victim deserves it or that abusive behavior is a part of any relationship. The decision to stay or leave an abusive relationship is often difficult. Victims need the support of their family and friends, and the help of community resources. With help, victims can become survivors when they escape their abusers. Better education of the public about IPV will help reduce the stigma it carries.

Jill Summers is glad to be back with her family and friends. She enjoys parties and the chance to give her grandma big hugs. She has a job and takes care of herself. Summers has always loved art and is finishing an online certificate in 3D animation. Jill says, "My advice for anyone in an abusive relationship is that if you break up the first time, stay broken up. You don't want to be like me and waste years with the wrong person."

Marielle Roberts works with a nonprofit organization dedicated to helping victims of domestic violence and educating the public about IPV. She recently finished her master's degree in social work. Marielle says, "My final piece of advice is to keep yourself as your own partner above anyone else. Believe in yourself first. Trust your own story first. That will never let you down."

# CHAPTER 6

# PTSD: COPING WITH THE STIGMA OF MILITARY-RELATED TRAUMA

Post-traumatic stress disorder (PTSD) occurs in people who have experienced or witnessed a traumatic event. Serious accidents, being a victim of a crime or rape, a near-death experience, or participating in combat can all lead to PTSD. While anyone of any age can develop PTSD, in the United States it most often occurs among military veterans. The traumatic events of war, involving bombs, grenades, gunfire, and death, are more than enough to cause PTSD. Nearly nine out of ten veterans have been exposed to potentially traumatic events.

## MILITARY PTSD

PTSD can be described as the past fighting with the present, but no one except the person with the disorder can see the

One study showed that about 13 percent of US veterans have been diagnosed with PTSD, nearly twice the rate as civilians. PTSD symptoms most often begin shortly after a traumatic event. But they may not appear for months or years. Then the symptoms can come and go for years or even a lifetime.

The National Center for PTSD of the Department of Veterans Affairs (VA) lists the four most common symptoms in veterans.

1. *Reliving the event*. Memories of the traumatic event can return at any time. The memories can feel frighteningly real and cause nightmares. You may experience flashbacks in which you feel as if you're living through the event again. A sight, sound, or smell may bring back bad memories. These are called triggers. Watching the news, seeing an accident, or hearing fireworks can trigger a flashback.

2. *Avoiding things that remind you of the event*. You may not want to think or talk about the traumatic event. You may avoid certain situations that remind you of what happened. For example, crowds may feel dangerous to you, or you may dislike driving if your traumatic event involved large groups of people or a vehicle.

3. *Having more negative thoughts and feelings than before the event*. Negative thoughts can make you feel numb and not want to see your friends or to do the activities you used to enjoy. It may feel as if the world is dangerous and if no one can be trusted. You may feel guilt and shame about the traumatic event, thinking you could have done more to prevent it, if only you'd tried harder or done something differently.

# BRIAN'S STORY

Brian Portwine joined the army when he was seventeen years old. After training, the army sent him to Baghdad, Iraq. During Portwine's two deployments in Iraq, he suffered numerous concussions and brain injuries.

But Portwine is no longer here to tell his story.

His mother, Peggy Portwine, spoke about her son in 2014 at a US House Committee on Veterans' Affairs hearing "Service Should Not Lead to Suicide: Access to VA's Mental Health Care." She and several other parents testified about their sons who had died of suicide after developing PTSD during deployments. The parents said their sons didn't receive the care they needed after they were discharged from the military.

Peggy Portwine testified, "My son, Specialist Brian Portwine, was an infantryman and served in Operation Iraqi Freedom in 2006–2008 and in Operation Enduring Freedom in 2010. While in Iraq in 2006, Brian was in a Bradley tank that was struck by an RPG [rocket-propelled grenade]. Brian suffered a blast concussion and had lacerations to his face and legs from shrapnel. This was Brian's first episode of traumatic brain injury [TBI]."

Peggy Portwine told the story of another mission in which her son and his sergeant were patrolling in a Humvee. An improvised explosive device (IED), or homemade bomb, hit the vehicle. The sergeant died in the blast, and her son was thrown from the Humvee. He was involved in seven similar attacks during his fifteen-month deployment.

"After coming home from his first deployment Brian had trouble with short term memory," Portwine explained. "When his friends were going somewhere he would often say, 'Where are we going again? You know I have scrambled brains.'"

In spite of Brian Portwine's numerous injuries during his first deployment, the army recalled him to Iraq in 2010. "During this deployment Brian did not email or call home or talk to his friends," Portwine said. "Little did we know how he was struggling with PTSD and TBI. He had panic attacks. He had nightmares three times a week. He suffered with anxiety, depression, insomnia, poor concentration, and hypervigilance. But he was never sent home."

When the army finally discharged Portwine in December 2010, he didn't want to return to college. Instead, he applied for disability assistance due to his PTSD and TBI but didn't tell anyone. "He knew the stigma of saying you had PTSD, so he kept it to himself," Portwine testified. "During out-processing from Fort Shelby [in Hattiesburg, Mississippi], Brian was diagnosed with PTSD, TBI, depression, and anxiety. During one assessment the counselor stated, 'Patient cannot remember questions asked.' Brian deteriorated quickly from December 2010 to May 2011. He could not stand how he acted but had no coping methods or treatment. If the DOD [Department of Defense] and VA assessed Brian at high risk for suicide, it is their duty to treat him. But he got nothing."

Brian Portwine took his own life on May 27, 2011. He was twenty-three years old. His obituary in an Atlanta newspaper stated, "In loving memory of Brian Lee Portwine, who bravely defended his country, receiving a purple heart and army commendation medal for his valiant service."

4. ***Feeling on edge or keyed up, a condition
   called hyperarousal.*** You may be jittery and
   always on alert, waiting for the worst to happen
   and getting ready for it. For example, you
   might suddenly become angry, have a hard
   time sleeping, be unable to concentrate, or be
   startled by loud noises. It's not uncommon for
   those with PTSD to act in unhealthy ways, such
   as using drugs or alcohol, smoking in excess, or
   driving recklessly.

Living with PTSD is difficult, and it can lead to suicide.
One study showed that 30,177 veterans and active-duty
personnel have died by suicide since the United States went
to war after the attacks on the World Trade Center and
Pentagon on September 11, 2001. That's more than four
times as many people as the 7,057 service members who
died in battle between September 2001 and June 2021.
Suicide is most common among veterans aged eighteen to
thirty-four. Veterans are also more likely to use guns during
suicide than civilians. According to a 2021 report from the
VA, more than seventeen veterans die from suicide each day
in the United States.

Will this trend slow down now that the US is no longer
involved in wars in the Middle East? The *New York Times*
reported, "The recent U.S. withdrawal from Afghanistan
may have marked the end of America's 'forever war,' but the
psychological fallout from two decades of military conflict
continues to reverberate among many of the 1.9 million
personnel who served overseas."

The rate of suicide among veterans who had received
care from the VA was far less than among those who had
no VA care, showing that PTSD can be treated with therapy
and medication. New treatments using psychedelic drugs

including psilocybin (made from certain mushrooms), ketamine (a medicine used in surgery that can cause forgetfulness), and MDMA (or ecstasy, which may produce positive feelings) are being tested. So far, they appear to have been effective in treating the symptoms of PTSD. As with other mental illnesses, successful treatment of PTSD can reduce the stigma associated with this condition.

Former army gunner Jose Martinez, who lost an arm and both of his legs to a roadside bomb in Afghanistan, strongly supports the use of psychedelic medications to treat PTSD. He told a reporter for the *New York Times*, "Psychedelics helped me realize that my problems are small compared to the world's bigger problems like starvation and cancer. And now I understand what I'm actually here for in this world, which is to make people smile and to remind them that life can be beautiful even when it's not so easy."

Help is available through the VA or the private sector. If you or someone you know suffers from military-related PTSD, call (800) 273-8255. Or access a live chat online at www .veteranscrisisline.net /get-help/chat.

## THE STIGMA OF PTSD

Author Corporal Trent Reedy fought in Afghanistan. Reedy learned about the reality of stigma associated with military-related PTSD during his service. He says, "To admit to any kind of mental or emotional health challenge in relation to the service was to destroy one's career. An NCO [noncommissioned officer] openly told us, in front of Army medical personnel, to lie and tell them we were fine,

## PTSD: ANYONE CAN GET IT

Anyone can develop PTSD after experiencing or witnessing a traumatic event. NAMI says the most common sources of trauma outside of the military that can cause PTSD include sexual assault or abuse, natural disasters, accidents and injuries, or a life-threatening situation. If people believe that only service members and veterans can develop PTSD, the recognition of symptoms and treatment can be delayed.

While half of all people experience at least one traumatic event during their lives, most won't develop PTSD. After a traumatic event, people are likely to have flashbacks or nightmares for a few weeks. But if those symptoms don't improve and they start to interfere with a person's life, it's time to seek help. If you have these symptoms for more than a month, you may have PTSD:

- flashbacks, bad dreams, frightening thoughts
- trying not to think about the experience, where it occurred, or what you felt like
- tension, anger, and sleep problems

Get help from a mental health professional as soon as possible for your PTSD. Different types of treatment such as cognitive behavioral therapy may help a person replace their negative thoughts and behaviors with positive ones. Exposure therapy can help a person face their fears and learn to cope with them. Early treatment is best, but it's never too late to seek help after a traumatic experience. Call the NAMI helpline at (800) 950-6264 or visit the website at https://www.nami.org/help and click "chat with us."

because admitting to trouble meant no promotions and no more deployments."

This sentiment aligns with Peggy Portwine's version of

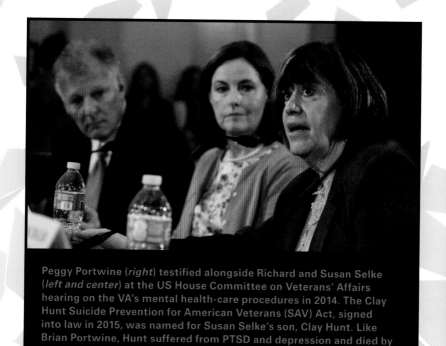

Peggy Portwine (*right*) testified alongside Richard and Susan Selke (*left and center*) at the US House Committee on Veterans' Affairs hearing on the VA's mental health-care procedures in 2014. The Clay Hunt Suicide Prevention for American Veterans (SAV) Act, signed into law in 2015, was named for Susan Selke's son, Clay Hunt. Like Brian Portwine, Hunt suffered from PTSD and depression and died by suicide after returning from military service in Iraq and Afghanistan.

the events that contributed to her son's suicide. "Up until the last few years the military culture has been that new recruits are molded as warriors during training and are told never to appear weak," Portwine explains. "Soldiers are afraid to report depression, anxiety, PTSD, suicidal thoughts, or nightmares because others in their unit may make fun of them or treat them differently. Soldiers are reluctant to seek help as it makes them seem as if they're not capable of doing their job." The public wants to see soldiers as brave and strong, and not weak in any way. That stereotype can cause difficulties in personal and work lives.

One medical journal found that common stereotypes of veterans with PTSD include the belief that these veterans are dangerous, violent, crazy, and responsible for their condition. Many veterans with PTSD report avoiding treatment so they wouldn't be labeled as mentally ill. Veterans with PTSD also commonly experience self-stigma. Peggy Portwine says,

> Another barrier to care is that when soldiers are arrested or in police custody, they are often incarcerated when what they need is treatment for PTSD. There are not enough VA centers to deal with depression, alcohol abuse, PTSD, TBI, and all the effects of war. The military ethos can be both a strength and a vulnerability. When soldiers share their experiences and feelings with each other, this helps them. The biggest barrier to care is a lack of reintegration programs after returning from war. If the military did three months of physical and mental testing and counseling when a service member is discharged, it could help reduce the stigma and suicides among veterans. It's more acceptable to have physical wounds because mental health wounds are invisible.

A report by the RAND National Defense Research Institute showed that stigma is a major reason many active-duty service members and veterans do not seek treatment for PTSD. Service members may believe that talking about mental health issues or seeking mental health care could affect their military careers. But not receiving treatment can be disastrous. Untreated PTSD can get worse and could have a major impact on a soldier's performance in combat or their ability to cope when they return home. It can also lead to much of the same prejudice and discrimination that people with other conditions such as addiction face every day. Key findings from the report include these:

- Mental health stigma involves service members and veterans internalizing feelings and beliefs about themselves. Typically, these feelings are negative beliefs that something is wrong with them if they are suffering from PTSD or other mental health disorders.
- Stigma for any reason can affect people's ability to cope with their lives and prevent them from seeking help. Stigma may affect people's well-being and quality of life, as well as the success of treatment.

## WOMEN VETERANS

Women also experience military-related PTSD and its stigma. Kayla Holst was in the military for eight years. She was part of the Marine Corps Motor Transportation unit and drove tanks and other vehicles to combat areas. She said, "When I got home, I didn't realize how [PTSD] would affect me. It affected me in a way that I never felt safe. . . . My brain remembered it like an IED blast. So, anything from a balloon popping or my mom hitting a curb with the car, my body would react as if I was back in my truck. I would sweat, have an immediate headache, and [become] incredibly irritated and [go on] very high alert. Sleeping by myself I assumed any noise I heard outside was an enemy combatant moving in on my truck."

In 1973 only 2 percent of military service members were women. By 2019 women made up 17 percent of military personnel. Women also face the stigma of PTSD. Women have legally only been able to fill any military role they quality for—including combat—since 2016. Stigma against women serving still has deep roots in the military, but it's decreasing as women prove they can successfully do the job.

But doing the job sometimes comes with PTSD, for women as well as for men. And PTSD sometimes leads to stigma, prejudice, and more discrimination. For example, some people believe that women don't belong in the military because "they can't do the same job as men do," they are not strong enough, or they are too emotional. That prejudice can lead to discrimination, such as lack of promotions and sexual harassment. One study showed that 54 percent of military women with PTSD were reluctant to seek care at a VA center because they worried it could affect their jobs, 47 percent worried that others would think

Women in the military often face more barriers to receiving the mental health care they need. In addition to the stigma of mental illness, woman service members may not have access to mental health professionals who understand gender-related needs and may lack knowledge of their eligibility for health care.

less of them, and 32 percent said they would think less of themselves for seeking the care they needed for PTSD.

## GETTING BETTER: REAL WARRIORS, REAL BATTLES, REAL STRENGTH

The Military Health System (MHS) is a form of nationalized health care that's part of the DOD. The MHS provides health care to active duty and reserve service members, retirees, veterans, and their dependents. The MHS established its Real Warriors Campaign to help service members and veterans cope with stigma and to minimize barriers to seeking the help they need. The campaign encourages service members, veterans, and military families who are coping with invisible wounds including PTSD to seek help without penalty. Part of the MHS's mission is to foster reaching out for help as a sign of strength, not weakness.

The Real Warriors Campaign promotes a culture of support for psychological health by encouraging the military community to seek help, whether for coping with the daily stresses of military life or for conditions such as depression, anxiety, and PTSD. The campaign acknowledges that self-stigma is often present in those with PTSD. The campaign's website reads, "Research shows that the stigma associated with psychological health concerns can keep service members from reaching out for help." To reduce stigma, the campaign recommends that military leaders

- create a unit culture of support and trust,
- speak openly with their unit,
- teach the importance of psychological health,
- connect directly with struggling warriors, and
- guide warriors to resources.

The website also offers tools for veterans, active-duty service members, family members, and providers. For example, it provides brochures describing steps to combat stigma and seek help. The campaign links service members, veterans, and their families to care, and provides free, confidential resources including online articles, print materials, videos, and podcasts. The organization also employs peer specialists—veterans who have experienced and recovered from a mental health condition caused by PTSD. These specialists are part of the treatment team and help design the recovery plan.

## THE PAST FIGHTING WITH THE PRESENT

While anyone can develop PTSD after a traumatic event, nearly 13 percent of American veterans develop it compared to about 7 percent of the civilian population. The thoughts and feelings that PTSD generates are difficult to live with. Both external and internal stigma can make a veteran with PTSD less likely to seek needed care. Yet it's vital that those with PTSD get the care they need. Treatment for PTSD includes therapy, medication, and support. The military's Real Warriors Campaign offers information, guidance, and peer counselors to help veterans with PTSD.

Peggy Portwine believes the VA has made good strides in providing treatment for PTSD and in decreasing the stigma associated with it. "There's still room for improvement," she says. So she continues her campaign. "Since testifying before Congress I've been active in the Iraq and Afghanistan Veterans of America," Portwine says. "I've done 'Out of the Darkness Walks' with the American Foundation for Suicide Prevention. A local television crew flew me to Washington, DC to support a bill that allowed veterans discharged with 'dirty papers' [less than honorable discharges due to PTSD] to appeal their discharge status. The bill passed. Many veterans who were abandoned with no mental health care were reinstated with benefits from the Veterans Affairs. We need to remember those lost in war, but we must also remember those who died due to its invisible wounds. Even though Brian came home, in his head he'd never left Iraq."

# CHAPTER 7

# DON'T FAT SHAME ME: MY WEIGHT IS NOT YOUR BUSINESS

Weight stigma is all too pervasive in American society, and it leads to ugly stereotypes. According to the World Obesity Federation, these stereotypes include the false beliefs that an overweight person is lazy, unattractive, not very intelligent, lacks will power and moral character, and has bad hygiene. These beliefs lead to widespread prejudice and discrimination against people perceived as being overweight. And our environment itself seems to send the same message. For example, seats in movie theaters and airplanes are not designed for larger individuals. This also happens in medical settings where wheelchairs, hospital gowns, and examination tables may not accommodate everyone.

Most Americans do weigh more than is recommended by health professionals. The average American woman is 5 feet 4 (1.6 m) and weighs just over 170 pounds (77 kg). The average American man is 5 feet 9 (1.8 m) and weighs 198 pounds (90 kg). While a person's weight impacts their health in many ways, weight stigma may be more damaging than extra weight. And it is important to note that all established measures for determining how much a person should weigh are flawed.

## THE SCOOP ON OBESITY

The word obese is a medical term, not a judgment of appearance. Obesity is a chronic disease where having too much body fat may—but not always—increase the risk for developing health problems. Some medical professionals use the body mass index (BMI) to categorize a person's weight. This figure is calculated using a person's height and weight. The average American man has a BMI of 26.6. The average American woman has a BMI of 26.5. This table shows the BMI for adults twenty years old and over.

| BMI | WEIGHT STATUS |
|---|---|
| Below 18.5 | Underweight |
| 18.5–24.9 | Normal |
| 25.0–29.9 | Overweight |
| 30 and higher | Obese to extremely obese |

# CATHERINE'S STORY

Catherine Felt struggled with her weight most of her life. "I was always the fat girl, even in junior high," she says. "The boys I had crushes on weren't interested in me because I wasn't pretty enough due to my weight. The stigma I felt heightened my insecurities about how I looked and made me insecure in other areas of my life. I remember people leaving notes in my locker saying that I was fat, and nobody would ever want to date me unless I lost weight. That went on all through high school."

Often people assume that overweight people are lazy or can't control what they eat. That happened to Felt. She explains, "I internalized those messages—that stigma—that people projected. Those words became part of my life. I don't remember anyone talking about my weight in a way that focused on helping me feel good about myself. That hurt my self-confidence. Even medical professionals seldom bothered beyond looking at my weight and pretty much ignored anything else that might be going on with my health."

When Felt turned twenty-five, she began to experience a lot of pain when she walked. She saw a podiatrist—a specialist in foot problems. He told Catherine she'd been born with short Achilles tendons, the tendons that connect leg muscles to the heel bone. That caused severe pain in her heels and feet, which kept her from exercising. The inability to exercise without pain made it more difficult for her to lose weight.

"I remember crying in the podiatrist's office when I realized I was not as lazy and weak as I had always been made to feel," Felt says. "I'd also been on medication that caused continual weight gain since I was an adult. Although physical therapy helped to keep my body healthier and reduce pain from my tendons, I knew that some people continued to make assumptions about my weight." It's a common misperception that heavier people live unhealthy lives that contribute to their weight. "But once I understood the medical reasons why I was continuing to gain weight, I could separate myself from the viewpoints of others and remind myself of the truth."

In 2018 Felt had gastric sleeve surgery in which surgeons remove about 80 percent of the stomach and join the remaining portions together. People can't eat as much as they did before the surgery, and they feel full more quickly. That can lead to rapid weight loss. Felt lost nearly half her body weight in the nine months following her surgery. But weighing too much was not Felt's primary reason for having this procedure.

**I decided on the surgery because the medications I'd been taking continued to pack on the pounds. And especially because I wanted to be a healthier mom and to live a long life. My doctor was very pleased that I lost as much weight as I did. This is much more than an appearance issue. I have a better quality of life now, and it means I can take my kids to the park. That's really important to me. Don't let anyone say that you cannot pursue your dreams because of your body. Be fearless and define yourself! Don't let yourself be the "fat person" in your own mind.**

For most people, BMI provides a fairly accurate measure of body fat, but it doesn't work for everyone. For example, a well-muscled athlete might be categorized as overweight based on BMI. While being overweight may be associated with greater risk of heart disease, the athlete is likely fit and healthy. Similarly, patients with hardly any muscle and a normal BMI may think they're healthy. But a lack of exercise can lead to poor heart health.

## KATELYN OHASHI'S STORY

Katelyn Ohashi competes for UCLA on January 21, 2019, nine days after her perfect-10 performance.

"I was told I looked like I'd swallowed an elephant, or looked like a pig," twenty-two-year-old gymnast Katelyn Ohashi said after she scored a perfect 10 on her floor routine at the 2019 Collegiate Challenge—a competition featuring top university gymnasts. Ohashi had been an Olympic hopeful as a teen, even beating her teammate Simone Biles in 2013. Soon after, several injuries ended Ohashi's promising career. But this was not her first brush with weight stigma.

Ohashi had experienced weight-related stigma as a child taking gym classes, and it worsened when she became an elite junior gymnast. She recalled in a blog post, "It started when I was thirteen, barely weighing seventy pounds [32 kg]. I had no option but to live up to the expectations of everyone else, so I experienced these cruel, unwanted body remarks from just about everyone—coaches, fans/

The standard BMI table doesn't work for kids and teens because children are continually growing during childhood and adolescence. The calculation of young people's BMI is based on age and gender, as well as height and weight. People nineteen and under can calculate their BMI using the formula at www.cdc.gov/healthyweight/bmi/calculator.html. The CDC says that more than 19 percent of children and teens are obese.

gymnastics followers, National team staff, my mother, and even myself."

After her injuries forced Ohashi to leave professional gymnastics, she wrote, "I have this sense of relief that I [won't] have to worry about getting in trouble about my weight or feeling self-conscious putting on a leotard in front of anyone." Within two months, Ohashi gained 20 pounds (9 kg). She said in her blog, "I have gained weight and gained it fast. I hate the way I look and feel. I feel like a failure, as though I am now actually everything I had ever been told. I feel as if my own mother cannot even look at me in the eyes, and now I am at the point I can't even look at myself."

Ohashi's life turned around when she entered the University of California, Los Angeles (UCLA). She joined the gymnastics team and represented UCLA at college competitions. In that gymnastics program, she became comfortable with her body. Ohashi said, "Everybody's bodies are different, and there's not a single body that is the perfect body. Being comfortable with the only person that matters—yourself—is something that you can forever work towards. You're the only person that has your back, and you're the only person that has your skin 100 percent of the time."

Being obese can lead to health problems. According to the CDC, obesity can

- increase blood pressure and cholesterol levels, risk factors for heart disease and strokes;
- lead to Type II diabetes; and
- increase the risk for cancer of the kidneys, liver, colon, breasts, and prostate; and lead to sleep apnea, a serious condition in which people stop breathing for a few seconds or minutes while sleeping.

Many factors contribute to being overweight or obese. Genetics is one factor. A medical journal found that 43 percent of the population has a gene called the fat mass and obesity-associated gene. People with this gene are prone to becoming overweight or obese but do not always develop it. Another major reason for a person becoming overweight

These college students are standing outside of a former Hy-Vee Mainstreet grocery store in Lincoln, Nebraska. When this grocery store closed in 2015, this area of Lincoln became a food desert. There were no grocery stores within a 1-mile (1.6 km) radius of this site. In 2015 Lincoln, Nebraska, had three food deserts, all in low-income areas.

or obese is the kind and amount of food they eat. Compared to some countries, processed food in the United States is relatively cheap, readily available, and often packed with far too many calories. The CDC finds that poverty can lead to obesity because poor people may not have the funds, time, or ability to buy and learn how to prepare healthful foods. And they are more likely than well-off people to live in a food desert, an area with limited access to grocery stores.

## WEIGHT STIGMA

People may be able to hide—at least temporarily—that they have an addiction or are mentally ill. But it's more difficult to hide the shape and size of your body. When people see an overweight person, they may make unfair assumptions about that person's health or lifestyle. Much like the stigma of addiction, the stigma of weight comes from the false belief that being overweight or obese is always a result of a person's poor choices or moral failure. People may believe that shame stemming from weight stigma will motivate overweight and obese people to lose weight. But shame is no motivator. Making assumptions and judgments about someone's health based on their appearance is an example of prejudice.

A person who struggles with the stigma of being overweight or obese may face further prejudice and discrimination from society. For example, doctors may pay too much attention to weight and not enough to other medical issues when an overweight person goes in for a checkup. Physicians often have less respect for patients with a higher BMI and generally spend less time talking to patients with obesity compared to their healthy-weight counterparts. One study showed that 53 percent of women received inappropriate comments from their doctor about their weight.

These stigmas start early. Nicole Avena is a neuroscientist

# HEALTH AT EVERY SIZE

The Association for Size Diversity and Health (ASDAH) envisions "a world that celebrates bodies of all shapes and sizes, in which body weight is no longer a source of discrimination, and where oppressed communities have equal access to the resources and practices that support health and well-being." People can be healthy—or unhealthy—at nearly any weight. One of ASDAH's primary beliefs is that "health status should never be used to judge, oppress, or determine the value of an individual." ASDAH's program, Health at Every Size, promotes several principles:

- *Weight inclusivity.* Accept and respect the diversity of body shapes and sizes.
- *Health enhancement.* Support policies that improve access to information and services that improve human well-being.
- *Eating for well-being.* Promote flexible, individualized eating plans based on hunger, nutritional needs, and pleasure, rather than eating plans focused on weight control.
- *Respectful care.* We must acknowledge our biases, work to end weight bias and stigma, and realize that socioeconomic status, race, gender, age, and other identities impact weight stigma.
- *Life-enhancing movement.* Support physical activities that allow people of all sizes, abilities, and interests to engage in enjoyable movement to the degree that they choose.

specializing in nutrition, diet, and addiction. Avena reported on two studies in *Psychology Today* that show that young people—like so much of society—often view overweight and obese individuals as impulsive, lazy, and less likable than people of "normal" weight. In one study, researchers showed children drawings of kids with different "handicaps" including children in wheelchairs, children with facial disfigurements, and obese children. The children liked the drawings of obese children less than the others.

Avena writes about a similar study, "High school girls had to decide how likeable they found photos of other girls. The photos of overweight girls were, once again, ranked last on their scale of likeability. However, when subjects were told that the overweight girls suffered from weight issues because of a thyroid problem, the photos of those overweight girls were liked just as much as the photos of normal-weight girls." She explains, "In the first condition, the overweight girls were their own perpetuators of their obesity, and in the second condition, the overweight girls were the victims of their condition."

Avena says, "When joining the fight against obesity, it is important to remember that many of the assumptions that we make toward obese children and adults are not true. There are many aspects of obesity that are controllable through diet and exercise, but we must not forget that obesity also has genetic and medical causes that are uncontrollable. Furthermore, the marketing of [high-sugar, high-fat foods] may keep many of us 'hooked' and always wanting more of these foods, regardless of whether we actually feel hungry."

## THE DOWNSIDE OF LOSING WEIGHT

Losing weight is not for everyone. Some people cannot and should not attempt to lose weight because of medical concerns or the need to take medications that cause weight gain. One study showed that up to half of adults with obesity have a low risk of developing additional health conditions. Up to 80 percent of people who lose a significant amount of weight regain it. And weight loss can result in decreased muscle mass. Regaining the weight—as most people do—results in more fat and not more muscle.

One study showed that women who intentionally lost at least 15 percent of their body weight were at twice the risk of death compared to overweight women whose weight remained stable. Another study of a group of people who lost over 22 pounds (10 kg) showed they were three and a half times more likely to die of heart disease compared to those who maintained a stable weight. Dieting can also be stressful and depressing, which can lead to a person eating more than before.

Some people decide that dieting is not worth it, that they can be happy and healthy at any weight. Lizzo, an award-winning singer, dancer, and songwriter, is one of those people. Lizzo had been subject to a lot of body-shaming during her career. But many consider her an icon for body positivity and self-confidence. She has given positive visibility to women considered by many to be overweight.

As Lizzo and her music gained fame, her body size became a topic of conversation. During an interview with *People* magazine, she said, "I know I'm fat. It doesn't bother me. I like being fat, and I'm beautiful and I'm healthy. I think I have a really hot body! I'm a body icon, and I'm embracing that more and more every day. What I'm doing is stepping into my confidence and my power to create my own beauty standard. And one day that will just be *the* standard."

Lizzo won an Emmy in 2022 for her internet streaming series, *Lizzo's Watch Out for the Big Grrrls*, in which thirteen women compete to dance with her. Like Lizzo, the women

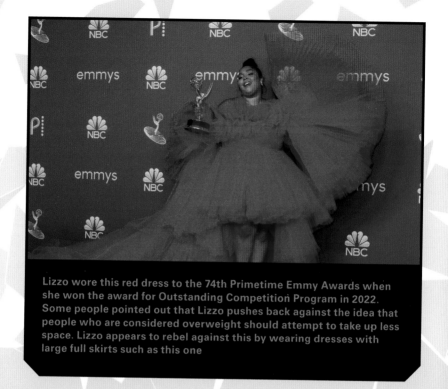

Lizzo wore this red dress to the 74th Primetime Emmy Awards when she won the award for Outstanding Competition Program in 2022. Some people pointed out that Lizzo pushes back against the idea that people who are considered overweight should attempt to take up less space. Lizzo appears to rebel against this by wearing dresses with large full skirts such as this one

were considered larger than the "typical" American woman. Lizzo is working toward the goal of normalizing bodies like hers. She says, "Inclusivity is what my message is always about."

One woman wrote in *Self*, an online magazine that specializes in women's health, beauty, and style, about her decision to stop trying to lose weight: "My name is Jes Baker, and I am a 300-pound [136 kg] person who is not trying to lose weight. I'm not trying to lose any weight, and I don't plan to in the foreseeable future." For many years Baker tried a dozen or more diets and just as many exercise programs. She said dieting robbed her of self-esteem, relationships, and experiences that she skipped for fear of being judged by her body, her peace of mind, her ability to trust herself, and her autonomy. "About five years ago I walked away from the lifestyle that caused more damage that I can calculate." She concluded her essay: "Recovery from the shame and self-loathing of diet culture is a hell of a journey and it often looks like a winding road with no end in sight. But for the first time in my life, I've decided to trust myself completely and embrace the fact that I am on a lengthy road, one that I might be on for a long time. That is a beautiful step towards healing in and of itself."

According to National Public Radio, diet culture is a set of social expectations that say there's only one way to look and only one way to eat, and that we are better and more worthy if our bodies look a certain way. And that way is thin. Diet culture is the idea that an overweight or obese person should force themselves to stick to a diet to lose weight. Many diets tell participants to restrict their food intake to an unsustainable level or cut out certain foods altogether. The inability or unwillingness to adhere to such a plan may cause self-stigma, or stigma from others because you are not as thin as "you should be." This stigma can have a greater impact on health than your weight. There are many resources for people who may be at risk for medical conditions because of their weight. People desiring or needing to lose weight for any reason should visit their doctors and follow their recommendations.

## THE BEST WEIGHT EVER

The stigma of being overweight or obese leads to stereotypes of laziness, unattractiveness, and unintelligence. These beliefs lead to widespread prejudice and discrimination in school, the workplace, and even in medical offices.

Do your part to decrease the stigma of weight. Use respectful language and be mindful and sensitive about the words used to refer to someone's weight. Speak up if you witness someone engaged in weight-based teasing or bullying. And educate others in your life about the stigma of weight and its harmful consequences. Helping people understand that obesity is a disease with complex causes can help stop harmful weight-based stereotypes. And remember that the best weight for everyone is the weight at which they are healthy, happy, and feel good about themselves.

After a divorce, Catherine Felt is now a single mother of two young children. In 2020 she worked on Kamala Harris's California presidential campaign. She's also an instructional assistant in a first-grade classroom. "I help kids with reading, math, and writing. We also work on developing social and emotional skills," she says. Felt will soon finish her BA in liberal arts and plans to get her teaching credentials after graduation. She recently updated her story: "I flew a few weeks ago and for the first time, I didn't feel like I was crowding anyone, nor did I need the seatbelt extension. It reminded me of victories I've made that are beyond what people think of my body. I feel better about myself and that makes all the difference."

Katelyn Ohashi graduated from UCLA in 2021, and she's devoting her time to photography, writing, and brand partnerships she's proud of. "There's not one thing that I don't enjoy doing, and it's a really exciting life to live." She continues to be involved in gymnastics and participated in the Gold Over America Tour featuring other well-known gymnasts. Ohashi is happier than ever. She said, "I'm a person that oozes joy and creative ideas. And I just want the best for everyone and myself."

# CHAPTER 8

# SMASHING THE STIGMA: WHAT YOU CAN DO

**N** ow that you know what stigma is and some of the ways it affects people's lives, you may wonder, "What can one person do?" You can do a lot, and you have already started by reading this book. Educating yourself about what stigma looks like for common conditions is the first step to reduce it. Only six categories of conditions are covered in this book. Think about other places you might see stigma in your life.

You can reject stereotypes. Question your automatic assumptions and judgments. When you have negative thoughts about someone or something, are your facts correct? Educate yourself about the various issues people face in their lives. Share that information with others. Keep a positive attitude about people you view as different and encourage other people to do the same. If someone asks you for help, think about what resources you can provide or refer them to an organization that supports people in their situation. Speak out if you see someone being discriminated against, especially for a stigmatized condition. Be open to hearing other people's stories.

To combat stigma, we must acknowledge that it exists. Combating stigma is a collective effort that involves all of us. The Obesity Action Coalition has some suggestions about weight stigma, but they also apply to other forms of stigma:

- Use respectful language when talking about people affected by any kind of stigma. Be mindful and sensitive about the words you use to refer to someone's weight, mental illness, addiction, lack of housing, or experience with intimate partner violence. Modeling respectful language is a way to show others how to do the same.
- Speak up if you witness someone teasing another person about their weight, addiction, mental illness, or other condition. Such jokes are not funny. They are harmful and reinforce stigma.
- If you are the target of prejudice or discrimination from family or friends, let them know their actions are hurtful and unfair.
- Educate others in your life about stigma and how it leads to stereotypes, prejudices, and discrimination. Help people understand that conditions such as mental illness, addiction, and obesity are diseases with complex causes.
- Does your school have an anti-bullying policy that protects students? If it doesn't, consider asking the school administrators to create one.

- If you work, does your workplace have an anti-harassment policy? Some companies may have committees that help address harassment in the workplace.
- When interacting with health-care providers, inform them of experiences you've faced in a health-care setting, including the way providers have talked to you about weight, addiction, mental illness, or other conditions you may be experiencing.

## LISTENING TO TEEN STORIES

After enduring a childhood filled with stigma, e.E. Charlton-Trujillo decided to take their fear and rage to the page and write a different ending for themselves. Their novel *Fat Angie* is about kids who face bullying, suicidal thoughts, issues of self-image and belonging, and questions of sexuality. They wrote in the Huffington Post, "Could this book be the foundation to inspire kids on the fringe to be their own difference through creative writing?"

In 2013 Charlton-Trujillo put their life on hold, rented a car, and set off on a four-month book tour across America that they called At-Risk Summer. During the tour, they planned to visit schools and community centers and encourage youth to express themselves through writing. They took camera gear with them to film the experience. Charlton-Trujillo wrote: "I rolled out of Cincinnati into the great unknown of winding roads, tornado weather, and every imaginable thing to challenge my phobias. All in an effort to empower at-risk youth through writing about themselves."

One stop on their tour was at a California high school where the students knew all about bullying and stigma. Charlton-Trujillo explained, "It's an alternative education school that harbors the kids deemed by many as the criminals, the rejects, and the misfits. These students inked with gang tattoos, dyed green punk hair, post teen pregnancies, or linebacker-sized guys with hidden identities who don't conform to the norm of traditional high school, soon became my heroes."

Charlton-Trujillo wanted the kids to write their stories, so they started by telling their own story: "I've been counted out more than I've been counted in. And I know that people have done the same to you. They've counted you out. But today you're counted in. Today you have a voice. You matter." Then they explained the writing prompt: *If Someone Only Knew . . .*

A boy Charlton-Trujillo called Mr. Quiet slumped at the back of the room. At first, he declined to tell his story, but then relented. "I'll go. I'll read," he said. "If someone only knew who I really am, they'd probably not see me the way they do. Most people just try to judge me by what they see. But only a few take the time to really listen to what I got to say. I am a person who wants to help a lot and would never leave someone in need."

As Charlton-Trujillo traveled across several states, the same thing happened repeatedly. Kids who had been beaten down by stigma came alive when someone cared about what they had to say. Charlton-Trujillo recalled in their article, "Kids on the fringe overcame the horrors of life and proved they are some of the bravest, most brilliant and enthusiastic youth. For those communities who still deem the youth I met as 'clearance kids,' I say, no markdowns are necessary. These kids are collectibles. Their value has yet to be set. Their stories represent a new American voice—the voices of those who can never be counted out." Listening to people who have experienced stigma is one of the ways you can start to dismantle it.

# MENTAL HEALTH STIGMA: NAMI CAN HELP

Are you ready to challenge your own thinking about the stigma of mental illness? NAMI offers a stigma quiz on their website. Take the quiz to discover what you really think.

1. **"I think people with mental illness . . ."**
   A. Need to snap out of it.
   B. Did something wrong to cause it.
   C. Need our love and support.
   D. Are sometimes faking it.

2. **Which of the following is not true about stigma?**
   A. It makes people feel alienated or feel "less than."
   B. It's not really a big problem for people with mental health conditions.
   C. It prevents people from seeking help for symptoms.
   D. It makes people fear judgment if they share their story.

3. **If someone in your family is diagnosed with a mental illness, you should:**
   A. Treat them differently than you used to.
   B. Distance yourself from them.
   C. Feel sorry for them.
   D. Listen to them and show support.

Question 1, Answer: C. People with mental illness need our love and support. Use respectful language to talk about mental health conditions. See the person, not the condition.
Question 2, Answer: B. Stigma *is* a big problem for people with mental health conditions; it affects their well-being and damages self-esteem.

Question 3, Answer: D. Tell your loved one you're there to help and you're not giving up on them. Learn as much as possible about your family member's condition. Listen carefully.

Consider taking NAMI's pledge to be stigma-free. While the pledge is directed toward those living with a mental illness, it also applies to other stigmatized conditions. "I promise to change my behavior to support everyone affected by mental health conditions. I will listen more and judge less. I won't use harmful words that prevent people from seeking help. I will be an ally to friends, family, and coworkers."

## MANAGING ADDICTION AND ITS STIGMA

Remember that addiction is in large part a brain disorder, often influenced by factors outside of a person's control. Three simple steps can help to reduce the stigma of addiction:

1. *Educate yourself*. Just as heart disease affects the body, addiction affects the brain. The causes of addiction are complex and due to many factors. Two good resources for more information are the National Institute on Drug Abuse and the Hazelden Betty Ford Foundation.
2. *Talk about addiction*. Discuss it with family members, friends, people who have an addiction, and people who work with those who have addictions. Talking helps to put a human face to the disease and shows that recovery is possible.
3. *Show compassion*. People with an addiction need your help and support, not shame and contempt. Strive to be a person your friends can count on.

The Hazelden Betty Ford Foundation is a nonprofit organization that has focused on addiction to alcohol and drugs for nearly seventy-five years. Their website says, "We are committed to challenging the stigma, stereotypes, and pessimism long associated with drug and alcohol addiction. Our fundamental addiction stigma-smashing strategy is to shine a light on people who are in recovery and, in doing so, expose the long-hidden reality that people actually do recover from drug and alcohol addiction; that it's a chronic disease that can be successfully managed for life; and that it affects individuals who are every bit as moral, productive, intelligent, talented—and humanly flawed—as the next person."

## HELPING THE UNHOUSED

After twenty years at Loaves & Fishes, Sister Libby Fernandez left in 2017 to establish Mercy Pedalers. The organization helps the unhoused and works to reduce the stigma of their condition. Sister Libby and a hundred volunteers pedal along the streets of Sacramento on tricycles equipped with cabinets and baskets looking for the unhoused. They carry hot coffee and chocolate, nutrition bars, hats and gloves, and hygiene items such as shampoo, toothbrushes, and toothpaste. When Mercy Pedalers meet an unhoused person, they first identify themselves and ask how they can help. The unhoused person might ask for a cup of coffee, a snack, or assistance to get into a shelter. "We try to provide everything essential to begin the trust and care in that relationship," Sister Libby says.

Sister Libby has some ideas for teens who want to help the unhoused. "Teens are so helpful. When they do community service through their school, they can come out with me or another Mercy Pedaler. They can organize a drive with their school to collect hygiene items, socks,

Sister Libby Fernandez (*left*) hands a bottle of water to an unhoused man during a heat wave in California.

and everything you need to give to the homeless on the streets."

Joseph Smith of Sacramento's Loaves & Fishes offers this advice: "Young people can be good citizens. Let your elected leaders know that a society where people live outside is not what you want for your world. They really do pay attention to young people. Ask, 'What are you doing about homelessness?' That can move officials to take notice."

## BE AWARE OF ABUSE AND VIOLENCE

February is Teen Dating Violence Awareness Month—a good time for you and your friends to think about other teens who may be in a bad relationship. Be aware of your peers and support them. Ask if something is going on in their personal lives. Offer encouragement and help anyone who is being abused to find a trusted adult, a teacher, a parent, a friend, or a health professional to talk with. Education in the school and community is the best way to fight the danger and stigma of intimate partner violence and abuse. Know the truth about these two myths:

1. *Myth*. "Domestic abuse always involves physical violence."
   *Truth*. Abusers control, threaten, and coerce their victims. Emotional and psychological abuse happen more often than physical violence and can be just as harmful.
2. *Myth*. "The victim brought it on themselves."
   *Truth*. Violence and abuse are never the fault of the victim. Be supportive and understanding. Never be judgmental.

## ADDRESSING PTSD STIGMA

After Peggy Portwine testified before Congress about PTSD and suicide, the government began to make changes. The DOD, the VA, and the military have taken steps to reduce the stigma associated with PTSD and to encourage people to seek help. Supporting those with mental health conditions is vital to address stigma and the prejudices and discrimination that come with it.

Remember, other events such as rape, assault, or a near-death experience can trigger PTSD. You can help by encouraging the person to talk about the traumatic experience and to seek professional help. Support people in your life who are working to recover from PTSD. It can be slow and difficult. As survivors recover from their

PTSD, they experience less stigma, which makes them feel better too.

Some psychiatrists suggest changing the term *post-traumatic stress disorder* to *post-traumatic stress injury* to help reduce the stigma. Using the word *injury* rather than *disorder* validates that severe reactions to traumatic events can be as much of an injury as a gunshot wound. This may help people understand that PTSD is a condition that may be cured or managed with treatment.

## FIGHT AGAINST WEIGHT STIGMA

People should not be defined or judged by their weight. Yet the stigma of weight is widespread and often doesn't consider that people can be healthy at any weight.

Smash the weight stigma by using respectful language when talking to or about someone who may be overweight or obese. Speak up if you hear someone fat-shaming another person. Do what you can to educate people about the stigma of weight and the dangerous stereotypes, prejudice, and discrimination it leads to. And if you realize you're the one having negative thoughts about a heavier person because of their appearance, stop and ask yourself why. Then focus on the person's positive attributes. Everyone has good qualities that have nothing to do with how they look. Maybe they're kind to animals and little kids, receive great grades, and work hard at everything they do.

The body positivity movement, which gained popularity in 2012, focuses on challenging unrealistic beauty standards regarding weight. It encourages people to appreciate and be confident about their bodies regardless of their appearance, and to accept their body's shape and size no matter how big or small, fat or thin. Everyone deserves to be treated with dignity and respect.

# REDUCING STIGMA FOR EVERYONE

Reducing stigma begins with you. Educate yourself about the stereotypes, prejudice, and discrimination that result from stigma. And remember that the six types in this book are not the only examples of stigma; with each example comes additional stereotypes, prejudices, and discriminatory practices. Be aware of your attitudes and actions. Choose your words carefully, because words have a big impact on others. Everyone has positive attributes so make it your goal to focus on the positive. Show compassion and support for everyone.

And if you feel you are on the receiving end of stigma, don't accept it. You are the only person who understands what's going on inside your head or in your life. The Mayo Clinic summarizes what we can do to cope with and reduce stigma:

- Don't let stigma create self-doubt and shame.
- Don't isolate yourself.
- Don't equate yourself with your condition. Try changing up the words you use. For example, you are not bipolar; you have bipolar disorder. You are not an addict; you have an addiction.
- Join a support group at school.

Speak out against stigma whenever you see it. Write a letter to the editor of your high school or local newspaper, use social media posts, and express your opinions in public as often as you can. You'll be helping everyone, including yourself.

Teens are more in touch with their feelings and are more sensitive to the feelings of others than in the past. They're often aware of the stigma they see every day at school, at home, and on social media. Many teens are working to recognize and lessen the stigma that they and their classmates face. As Catherine Felt reminds us, "You can overcome stigma because you are a person of electrifying possibilities. Find your passions and don't let anyone say that you cannot pursue them. Be fearless. Be the one who defines yourself."

# GLOSSARY

**addiction:** a condition in which the repeated use of a drug or alcohol leads to extreme craving for the drug. The long-term use of the drug changes brain chemistry and makes it difficult to stop using the drug without experiencing painful withdrawal symptoms.

**anxiety:** a sense of uneasiness, nervousness, worry, fear, or dread of what's about to happen or what might happen. Humans feel fear in the presence of danger, but anxiety is worrying about danger even when it is not present.

**bipolar disorder:** a mental condition in which moods swing between extremes of low depression and manic highs. Episodes of both lows and highs can last from days to months. Treatment includes medication and therapy.

**body mass index (BMI):** a formula that estimates a person's body fat based on height and weight. The BMI tables range from underweight to normal to overweight to obesity. It is a helpful, but not definitive, predictor of health.

**depression:** a mental condition involving feeling sad, down, or numb most of the time to the point that it affects how a person thinks and acts. Depression causes a loss of interest in people and activities that used to be enjoyable.

**discrimination:** actions taken against people based on stereotypes and prejudice. Discrimination can include behaviors such as refusing to live near or work with someone different from you.

**domestic violence:** see intimate partner violence

**homeless:** an outdated term for someone lacking a permanent home. See unhoused.

**intimate partner violence (IPV):** violence committed by someone in the victim's domestic circle, such as a partner, ex-partner, or family member. It can be physical, sexual, or emotional abuse. Anyone can be a victim, but it most often involves a male partner abusing his female partner.

**mental health:** the condition of one's psychological and emotional well-being

**mental illness:** a wide range of conditions that affect mood, emotions, thinking, and behavior that may cause unhappiness and problems functioning in normal activities

**obesity:** a condition characterized by the excessive accumulation and storage of fat in the body

**obsessive-compulsive disorder (OCD):** a mental condition in which people have recurring, unwanted thoughts, ideas, or sensations (obsessions) that make them feel driven to do something repetitively (compulsions). This could include frequent handwashing or checking doors repeatedly to be sure they are locked.

**opioid:** a drug such as the illegal drug heroin, a synthetic opioid such as fentanyl, a pain reliever available legally by prescription, such as oxycodone, hydrocodone, codeine, and many others

**post-traumatic stress disorder (PTSD):** a mental condition caused by a terrifying event, with symptoms such as nightmares, severe anxiety, and flashbacks to the traumatic event. It can happen to anyone who experiences trauma, but it is most often seen in veterans who have been in armed conflicts.

**prejudice:** preconceived negative beliefs about large groups of people who fit a stereotype, such as those with mental illness or those of a different race or religion from your own. Prejudice often leads to discrimination.

**psychosis:** a mental condition in which a person experiences episodes that cause abnormal thinking and perceptions. During such an episode, the person loses touch with reality and may see and hear things that are not there.

**self-stigma:** a mark of shame or disgrace that people internalize about themselves as a result of what others say or believe about them

**stereotype:** putting individual people who may have similar traits into groups. Stereotypes are oversimplified and mistaken ideas about a group of people based on how they look or how they act.

**stigma:** a false idea that can lead to negative beliefs about a person's perceived characteristics that can result in harmful actions

**traumatic brain injury (TBI):** injuries to the brain caused by being hit in the head, falling, or being shot in the head by a bullet. TBIs range from headaches to mild concussions to comas or death.

**unhoused:** without a permanent home. Unhoused people may live in tents, sleep on the ground, or find temporary housing at a shelter.

# SOURCE NOTES

5   "I've had this . . . and for them.": Brandon Brooks, quoted in Tim
    McManus, "Anxiety-Related Illness Forced Eagles RG Brandon Brooks
    out of Game," *ESPN*, November 25, 2019, https://www.espn.com
    /nfl/story/_/id/28160877/anxiety-related-illness-forced-eagles-rg
    -brandon-brooks-game.

9   "alienated and seen . . . always pursue opportunities.": "StigmaFree
    Me," National Alliance on Mental Illness, accessed November 15,
    2022, https://www.nami.org/Get-Involved/Pledge-to-Be-StigmaFree
    /StigmaFree-Me.

11  "I think now . . . on in Paris.": Naomi Osaka, quoted in Matthew
    Futterman, "Naomi Osaka Quits the French Open after News
    Conference Dispute," *New York Times*, May 31, 2021, https://www
    .nytimes.com/2021/05/31/sports/tennis/naomi-osaka-quits-french
    -open-depression.html.

11  "It's O.K. to not be O.K.": Naomi Osaka, "Naomi Osaka: 'It's O.K. Not
    to Be O.K,'" *Time*, July 8, 2021, https://time.com/6077128/naomi
    -osaka-essay-tokyo-olympics/.

11  "At the end . . . us to do": Simone Biles, quoted in Juliet Macur,
    "Simone Biles Said She Was Not in a Good Place Mentally to
    Continue," *New York Times*, July 27, 2021, https://www.nytimes
    .com/2021/07/27/sports/olympics/russia-wins-gold-medal
    -gymnastics.html.

11  "I stuffed my . . . with their emotions.": Michael Phelps, quoted in
    Eileen Finan, "Michael Phelps on Why It's 'Challenging' for Athletes to
    Admit Their Mental Health Struggles," *People*, July 8, 2021, https://
    people.com/sports/michael-phelps-on-why-its-challenging-for
    -athletes-to-admit-their-mental-health-struggles/.

11  "[Biles] opening up . . . of the water.": Michael Phelps, quoted in KC
    Baker, "Simone Biles Is 'Blowing the Stigma Surrounding Mental
    Health Out of the Water,' Says Michael Phelps," *People*, November
    11, 2021, https://people.com/sports/michael-phelps-simone-biles
    -mental-health-stigma/.

12  "I am not good enough.": "What Is Stigma?" Wisconsin Initiative for
    Stigma Elimination (WISE). July 15, 2017, https://wisewisconsin.org
    /blog/what-is-stigma/.

12 "One thing people . . . in their abuse.": Chris Crutcher, interview with the author, August 15, 2021.

12–13 "I was an . . . my sexual orientation": e.E. Charlton-Trujillo, personal interviews with the author, September 2021.

14–16 "A basketball hit . . . that is dangerous.": Charlton-Trujillo.

14 "Sadly, stigma is . . . might be contagious.": Ann Steiner, personal interviews with the author, October 2019 and September 2021.

14–15 "Stigma comes in . . . what therapy is.": Steiner.

16 "Stigmas related to . . . our personal traumas.": Charlton-Trujillo, interviews.

16–17 "The stigma that . . . its own tail.": Crutcher, interview.

20 "I was in . . . still go wrong.": Amanda Lipp, interview with the author, October 27, 2021.

20–21 "Group therapy didn't . . . share their story.": Lipp.

25–26 "Rather than receiving . . . severe mental illness.": Esmé Weijun Wang, *The Collected Schizophrenias* (Minneapolis: Graywolf, 2019), 73.

26 "High school can . . . about to end.": Hailey Hardcastle, quoted in William Wan, "Schools Now Letting Students Stay Home Sick for Mental-Health Days," *Washington Post*, October 22, 2019, https://www.washingtonpost.com/health/schools-now-letting-youths-stay-home-sick-for-mental-health-days/2019/10/21/15df339a-e93b-11e9-85c0-85a098e47b37_story.html.

28 "The stigma of . . . it to yourself.": Lipp, interview.

30 "People with a . . . emergency room visits.": Adapted from "The Ripple Effect of Mental Illness," National Alliance on Mental Illness, accessed November 15, 2022, https://www.nami.org/NAMI/media/NAMI-Media/Infographics/NAMI_Impact_RippleEffect_2020_FINAL.pdf.

31 "The barbershop is . . . without being judged.": Trey Cato, quoted in Hilary Powell, "How Barbers Are Cutting Mental Health Stigma among Black Men," Side Effects Public Media, December 3, 2020, https://www.sideeffectspublicmedia.org/community-health/2020-12-03/how-barbers-are-cutting-mental-health-stigma-among-black-men.

31  "My shop is . . . to speak life.": Cato, quoted in Powell.

31  "When our patrons . . . you been depressed.'": James Garrett Jr., quoted in Powell.

31–32  "Minorities are often . . . require professional care.": Jeanne Miranda, quoted in "Top 5 Barriers to Mental Healthcare Access," Social Solutions, accessed November 5, 2021, https://www.socialsolutions .com/blog/barriers-to-mental-healthcare-access/.

33  "Now I feel . . . who I am.": Lipp, interview.

34  "The four of . . . for a meal.": Donna Kull and Brian Kull, interviews with the author, February 28–March 5, 2016.

34–35  "The call that . . .No, not Adam!'": Kull and Kull, interview, October 26, 2021.

35  "I said that . . . to Adam's apartment.": Kull and Kull.

37  "To feel good. . . . to do so.": Adapted from "Drug Misuse and Addiction," National Institute on Drug Abuse, July 13, 2020, https:// nida.nih.gov/publications/drugs-brains-behavior-science-addiction /drug-misuse-addiction.

38–39  "The initial decision . . . hallmark of addition.": "Understanding Drug Use and Addiction DrugFacts," National Institute on Drug Abuse, June 6, 2018, https://nida.nih.gov/publications/drugfacts /understanding-drug-use-addiction.

40  "I was extremely . . . my life—opioids.": Alisha Choquette, interviews with the author, October 2021.

40  "I remember the . . . lengths to chase.": Choquette.

40–41  "By the end . . . they were gone.": Choquette.

41  "I kept telling . . . just grew stronger.": Choquette.

42  "Being a drug . . . with each relapse.": Choquette.

43  "Medical care is . . . entrenches their disease.": Nora Volkow, quoted in "Addressing the Stigma That Surrounds Addiction," *Nora's Blog*, National Institute on Drug Abuse, April 22, 2020, https://www .drugabuse.gov/about-nida/noras-blog/2020/04/addressing-stigma -surrounds-addiction.

44    "There's a stigma . . . these friendships ended.": Kull and Kull, interview, October 26, 2021.

45    "I believe we . . . that I've become.": Choquette, interview.

47    "The label of . . . the first place.": "Why Unhoused?," Unhoused.org, accessed December 3, 2021, https://www.unhoused.org/overview.

47    "We've seen this . . . to be retired.": Eve Garrow, quoted in Nicholas Slayton, "Time to Retire the Word 'Homeless' and Opt for 'Houseless' or 'Unhoused' Instead?," *Architectural Digest*, May 21, 2021, https://www.architecturaldigest.com/story/homeless-unhoused.

47, 50    "[The number of . . . very serious issue.": Sister Libby Fernandez, "Mercy Pedalers Founder Sister Libby," interview by Stu VanAirsdale, *Sactown Magazine*, November 2019, https://www.sactownmag.com/mercy-pedalers-founder-sister-libby/.

48    "One day I . . . my homeless years.": Joseph David Smith, interview with the author, December 20, 2021.

48    "I was an . . . the time before.": Smith.

49    "And there I . . . severe liver damage.": Smith.

49    "Alcoholism is a . . . been my rock.": Smith.

49    "After I'd been . . . more stable environment.": Smith.

49    "shake the cobwebs": Smith.

50    "There's a lot . . . that is tough.": Smith.

50    "You can engage . . . not the person.": Smith.

51    "housing on which . . . costs, including utilities.": "Glossary of Terms to Affordable Housing," U.S. Department of Housing and Urban Development, accessed December 5, 2021, https://archives.hud.gov/local/nv/goodstories/2006-04-06glos.cfm.

55    "Homeless people are . . . old or disabled.": Adapted from Romeo Vitelli, "Why Is Homelessness So Stigmatized?," *Psychology Today*, June 5, 2021, https://www.psychologytoday.com/us/blog/media-spotlight/202106/why-is-homelessness-so-stigmatized.

56    "The biggest thing . . . and getting respect.": Sister Libby Fernandez, interview with the author, November 16, 2021.

56–57   "In most cases . . . to get breakfast.": Maralyn Soifer, interview with the author, January 19, 2022.

57   "Teachers would assign . . . and other supplies.": Soifer.

57   "We often lost . . . at our school.": Soifer.

57   "Elementary-aged children could . . . drive at school.": Soifer.

61   "Now I'm the . . . to help them.": Smith, interview.

63   "Anyone can be . . . and all lifestyles.": "Dynamics of Abuse," National Coalition Against Domestic Violence, accessed December 12, 2021, https://ncadv.org/dynamics-of-abuse.

64   "When we first . . . my first love.": Jill Summers, interview with the author, January 13, 2022.

64   "I had a . . . a virgin anymore.": Summers.

64–65   "Every time I . . . anyone but him.": Summers.

65   "He'd hold me . . . I could do.": Summers.

65   "Lucas called me . . . the final straw.": Summers.

65   "I didn't tell . . . all those years.": Summers.

66   "It wasn't love . . . often lethal combination.": Marielle Roberts, interview with the author, December 2, 2021.

66–67   "Someone I loved . . . know he is.": Roberts.

66–68   "*Physical abuse*. Hitting, . . . on an allowance.": Adapted from "Types of Abuse," Women Against Violence, accessed November 12, 2022, https://www.womenagainstabuse.org/education-resources/learn-about-abuse/types-of-domestic-violence.

67   "When I talked . . . my self-blame sooner.": Roberts, interview.

67   "While my anger . . . And it was.": Roberts.

70   "Intimate partner violence . . . for their injuries.": Adapted from "Statistics," National Coalition Against Domestic Violence, accessed November 15, 2022, https://ncadv.org/statistics.

71   "For me, I . . . his horrible words.": Anonymous woman, interview with the author, December 15, 2021.

71 "The fear of . . . on their abuser.": Marc L'Ecluse, interview with the author, January 6, 2022.

73 "It requires incredible . . . ask for help.": L'Ecluse.

74 "Nearly 44 percent . . . identified as bisexual.": Adapted from "Domestic Violence and the LGBTQ Community," National Coalition Against Domestic Violence, June 6, 2018, https://ncadv.org/blog /posts/domestic-violence-and-the-lgbtq-community.

75 "Physicians should learn . . . victims of IPV.": Ping-Hsin Chen, Abbie Jacobs, and Susan L. D. Rovi, "Intimate Partner Violence: IPV in the LGBT Community," National Library of Medicine, September 2013, https://pubmed.ncbi.nlm.nih.gov/24053263/.

76 "Heart Heavy as . . . words never again.": Meggie Royer, "Heart Heavy as a Fist," *Writings for Winter* (blog), *Tumblr*, March 13, 2013, https://writingsforwinter.tumblr.com/post/45323636045/heart-heavy -as-a-fist.

77 "We hear from . . . experiencing abuse. Nothing.": Sara Grady, quoted in "Stigma Impacts Domestic Violence Survivors," Erie County Anti Stigma Coalition, accessed October 5, 2021, https://letstalkstigma .org/stigma-impacts-domestic-violence-survivors/.

77 "Many victims of . . . treatment for years.": Wendy L. Patrick, "How Social Stigma Silences Domestic Violence Victims," *Psychology Today*, April 9, 2018, https://www.psychologytoday.com/us/blog/why-bad -looks-good/201804/how-social-stigma-silences-domestic-violence -victims.

79 "My advice for . . . the wrong person.": Summers, interview.

79 "My final piece . . . let you down.": Roberts, interview.

81, 84 "Reliving the event. . . . or driving recklessly.": Adapted from "PTSD Basics," U.S. Department of Veteran Affairs, last modified November 8, 2022, https://www.ptsd.va.gov/understand/what/ptsd_basics.asp.

82 "My son, Specialist . . . brain injury [TBI].": Peggy Portwine, testimony, House Committee on Veterans' Affairs, accessed October 25, 2021, https://archives-veterans.house.gov/witness-testimony/peggy -portwine.

82–83 "After coming home . . . have scrambled brains.'": Portwine.

83 "During this deployment . . . never sent home.": Portwine.

83 "He knew the . . . he got nothing.": Portwine.

83 "In loving memory . . . his valiant service.": Brian Portwine, obituary, June 5, 2011, *Atlanta Journal-Constitution*, https://www.legacy.com /us/obituaries/atlanta/name/brian-portwine-obituary?id=26365912.

84 "The recent U.S. . . . who served overseas.": Andrew Jacobs, "Veterans Have Become Unlikely Lobbyists in Push to Legalize Psychedelic Drugs," *New York Times*, November 11, 2021, https:// www.nytimes.com/2021/11/11/health/veterans-psychedelics-ptsd -depression.html.

85 "Psychedelics helped me . . . not so easy.": Jose Martinez, quoted in Jacobs.

85–86 "To admit to . . . no more deployments.": Trent Reedy, interview with the author, December 14, 2021.

87 "Up until the . . . doing their job.": Peggy Portwine, interview with the author, December 5, 2021.

88 "Another barrier to . . . wounds are invisible.": Portwine.

89 "When I got . . . on my truck.": Kayla Holst, quoted in Natasha Lynn, "Ending the Stigma behind Post-Traumatic Stress Disorder for PTSD Awareness Month in June," KKCO, July 27, 2021, https://www .nbc11news.com/2021/06/28/ending-stigma-behind-post-traumatic -stress-disorder-ptsd-awareness-month-june/.

91 "Research shows that . . . out for help.": "5 Ways Military Leaders Can Address Stigma," Military Health System, Real Warriors Campaign, June 23, 2021, https://health.mil/Reference-Center/Publications /2021/06/23/5-Ways-Military-Leaders-Can-Address-Stigma-Fact -Sheet.

91 "create a unit . . . warriors to resources.": Adapted from "5 Ways Military Leaders Can Address Stigma."

92–93 "There's still room . . . never left Iraq.": Portwine, interview.

96 "I was always . . . through high school.": Catherine Felt, interview with the author, January 12, 2022.

96 "I internalized those . . . with my health.": Felt.

97 "I remember crying . . . of the truth.": Felt.

97 "I decided on . . . your own mind.": Felt.

98 "I was told . . . like a pig": Katelyn Ohashi, quoted in Sophie Gallagher, "Gymnast Katelyn Ohashi Says She Was Body-Shamed Online after Perfect 10 Routine," HuffPost, updated May 23, 2019, https://www .huffingtonpost.co.uk/entry/gymnast-katelyn-ohashi-says-she-was -body-shamed-online-after-perfect-10-routine_uk_5ce65667e4b05 47bd13280da.

98–99 "It started when . . . and even myself.": Katelyn Ohashi, blog, accessed September 14, 2021, https://katelyn-ohashi.com/category /athlete-body-shaming/.

99 "I have this . . . look at myself.": Ohashi.

99 "Everybody's bodies are . . . of the time.": Katelyn Ohashi, quoted in Becky Grey et al., "I Was Told I Looked like a Pig'—Viral Gymnastic Star Katelyn Ohashi's Battles with Body Image," BBC Sports, May 23, 2019, https://www.bbc.com/sport/48340080.

102 "a world that . . . health and well-being.": "About the Association for Size Diversity and Health (ASDAH)," Association for Size Diversity and Health, accessed October 21, 2021, https://asdah.org/about-asdah/.

102 "health status should . . . of an individual.": "HAES Principles," Association for Size Diversity and Health, accessed October 21, 2021, https://asdah.org/health-at-every-size-haes-approach/.

102 "Weight inclusivity. Accept . . . that they choose.": Adapted from "HAES Principles."

103 "High school girls . . . of their condition.": Nicole Avena, "The Obesity Stigma: The Negative Social Consequences of Being Obese," *Psychology Today*, June 12, 2013, https://www.psychologytoday.com /us/blog/food-junkie/201306/the-obesity-stigma.

103 "When joining the . . . actually feel hungry.": Avena.

104 "I know I'm . . . be *the* standard.": Lizzo, quoted in Jason Sheeler, "Lizzo on Blazing Her Own Path, Finding Her 'Power' and Shutting Down Body Shamers: 'I'm a Body Icon,'" *People*, March 2, 2022, https://people.com/music/lizzo-women-changing-the-world-people -cover-story/.

105     "Inclusivity is what . . . is always about.": Lizzo, quoted in Claudia Rankine, "Lizzo on Hope, Justice, and the Election," *Vogue*, September 24, 2020, https://www.vogue.com/article/lizzo-cover-october-2020.

105–106     "My name is . . . and of itself.": Jes Baker, quoted in "Nope, I'm Not Trying to Lose Weight," Self, June 26, 2018, https://www.self.com/story/im-not-trying-to-lose-weight.

107     "I help kids . . . and emotional skills": Felt, January 12, 2022.

107     "I flew a . . . all the difference.": Felt, May 21, 2022.

107     "There's not one . . . everyone and myself.": Katelyn Ohashi, quoted in Samantha Brodsky, "Gymnastics Icon Katelyn Ohashi Is Thriving 2 Years after Graduating from UCLA," Pop Sugar, June 16, 2021, https://www.popsugar.com/fitness/where-is-katelyn-ohashi-now-48373804.

109–110     "Use respectful language . . . may be experiencing.": Adapted from Rebecca Puhl, "Combating Weight Bias: Why We Need to Take Action," Obesity Action Coalition, accessed November 15, 2022, https://www.obesityaction.org/resources/combating-weight-bias-why-we-need-to-take-action/.

110     "Could this book . . . through creative writing?": e.E. Charlton-Trujillo, "The Clearance Kids," HuffPost, updated April 13, 2014, https://www.huffpost.com/entry/the-clearance-kids_b_4763105.

110     "I rolled out . . . writing about themselves.": Charlton-Trujillo.

110–111     "It's an alternative . . . became my heroes.": Charlton-Trujillo.

111     "I've been counted . . . voice. You matter.": Charlton-Trujillo.

111     "I'll go. I'll . . . someone in need.": Charlton-Trujillo.

111     "Kids on the . . . be counted out.": Charlton-Trujillo.

112–113     "I think people . . . condition. Listen carefully.)": Adapted from "StigmaFree Quiz Results," National Alliance on Mental Illness, accessed October 5, 2021, https://www.nami.org/Get-Involved/Pledge-to-Be-StigmaFree/StigmaFree-Me/StigmaFree-Quiz-Results.

113     "I promise to . . . family, and coworkers.": "StigmaFree Quiz Results."

114    "We are committed . . . the next person.": "Smashing the Stigma of Addiction," Hazelden Betty Ford Foundation, accessed October 7, 2021, https://www.hazeldenbettyford.org/recovery-advocacy/stigma-of-addiction#.

114    "We try to . . . in that relationship": Fernandez, interview.

114–115    "Teens are so . . . on the streets.": Fernandez.

115    "Young people can . . . to take notice.": Smith, interview.

118    "Don't let stigma . . . group at school.": Adapted from "Mental Health: Overcoming the Stigma of Mental Illness," Mayo Clinic, accessed November 15, 2021, https://www.mayoclinic.org/diseases-conditions/mental-illness/in-depth/mental-health/art-20046477.

119    "You can overcome . . . who defines yourself.": Felt, interview.

# SELECTED BIBLIOGRAPHY

Charlton-Trujillo, e.E. "The Clearance Kids." HuffPost. Last modified April 13, 2014. https://www.huffpost.com/entry/the-clearance-kids_b_4763105.

"Childhood Obesity Facts." CDC, April 5, 2021. https://www.cdc.gov/obesity/data/childhood.html.

"Drug Misuse and Addiction." National Institute on Drug Abuse. Accessed November 2, 2021. https://nida.nih.gov/publications/drugs-brains-behavior-science-addiction/drug-misuse-addiction.

"Dynamics of Abuse." National Coalition Against Domestic Violence. Accessed November 2, 2021. https://ncadv.org/dynamics-of-abuse.

"Effects of Domestic Violence on Children." Office on Women's Health, April 2, 2019. https://www.womenshealth.gov/relationships-and-safety/domestic-violence/effects-domestic-violence-children.

Fernandez, Sister Libby. "Mercy Pedalers Founder Sister Libby." Interview by Stu VanAirsdale. *Sactown Magazine*, November 2019. https://www.sactownmag.com/mercy-pedalers-founder-sister-libby/.

"5 Barriers to Mental Health Treatment and Access to Care." Social Solutions, May 4, 2022. https://www.socialsolutions.com/blog/barriers-to-mental-healthcare-access/.

"Five Steps to Lose Weight and Keep It Off." American Heart Association, January 9, 2017. https://www.heart.org/en/healthy-living/healthy-eating/losing-weight/5-steps-to-lose-weight-and-keep-it-off.

Gallagher, Sophie. "Gymnast Katelyn Ohashi Says She Was Body-Shamed Online after Perfect 10 Routine." HuffPost. Updated May 23, 2019. https://www.huffingtonpost.co.uk/entry/gymnast-katelyn-ohashi-says-she-was-body-shamed-online-after-perfect-10-routine_uk_5ce65667e4b0547bd13280da.

"HUD: Growth of Homelessness during 2020 Was 'Devastating,' Even before the Pandemic." National Public Radio, March 18, 2021. https://www.npr.org/2021/03/18/978244891/hud-growth-of-homelessness-during-2020-was-devastating-even-before-the-pandemic.

"Losing Weight: Getting Started." CDC, November 24, 2021. https://www.cdc .gov/healthyweight/losing_weight/getting_started.html.

"Native and Indigenous Communities and Mental Health." Mental Health America. Accessed January 11, 2023. https://www.mhanational.org/issues/native -and-indigenous-communities-and-mental-health.

"Obesity." Mayo Clinic. Accessed November 25, 2021. https://www.mayoclinic .org/diseases-conditions/obesity/symptoms-causes/syc-20375742.

"Obesity and Genetics." Obesity Medicine Association, July 23, 2018. https:// obesitymedicine.org/obesity-and-genetics/.

Patrick, Wendy L. "How Social Stigma Silences Domestic Violence Victims." *Psychology Today*, April 9, 2018. https://www.psychologytoday.com/us/blog/why -bad-looks-good/201804/how-social-stigma-silences-domestic-violence-victims.

Powell, Hilary. "How Barbers Are Cutting Mental Health Stigma among Black Men." WFYI Public Media, December 3, 2020. https://www.sideeffectspublic media.org/community-health/2020-12-03/how-barbers-are-cutting-mental -health-stigma-among-black-men.

"Preventing Teen Dating Violence." CDC, March 5, 2021. https://www.cdc.gov /violenceprevention/intimatepartnerviolence/teendatingviolence/fastfact.html/.

"PTSD Basics." US Department of Veterans Affairs. Accessed September 24, 2001. https://www.ptsd.va.gov/understand/what/ptsd_basics.asp.

"Quick Guide: Teen Dating Violence." National Coalition Against Domestic Violence, February 7, 2017. https://ncadv.org/blog/posts/quick-guide-teen -dating-violence.

"Service Should Not Lead to Suicide." Congressional Committee on Veterans' Affairs. Written testimony of Peggy Portwine, July 10, 2014. https://www.govinfo .gov/content/pkg/CHRG-113hhrg89378/html/CHRG-113hhrg89378.htm.

"Smashing the Stigma of Addiction." Hazelden Betty Ford Foundation. Accessed October 3, 2021. https://www.hazeldenbettyford.org/recovery-advocacy/stigma -of-addiction.

"State of Homelessness: 2021 Edition." National Alliance to End Homelessness. Accessed September 9, 2021. https://endhomelessness.org/homelessness-in -america/homelessness-statistics/state-of-homelessness-2021/.

"Weight Stigma." World Obesity Federation. Accessed September 19, 2021. https://www.worldobesity.org/what-we-do/our-policy-priorities/weight-stigma.

"What Is Stigma?" Wisconsin Initiative for Stigma Elimination (WISE), July 15, 2017. https://wisewisconsin.org/blog/what-is-stigma/.

"Why Do Victims Stay?" National Coalition Against Domestic Violence. Accessed September 21, 2021. https://ncadv.org/why-do-victims-stay.

# FURTHER INFORMATION

## Books

Casey, Michael. *Breaking Free: A Compilation of Short Stories on Mental Illness and Ways to Handle Them*. Rochestown, Cork, Ireland: Orla Kelly Self-Publishing Services, 2019.
Mental health stigma is very real. This book discusses a dozen or more mental conditions and how to overcome them. It contains an intriguing mix of facts and fictional stories of people with addiction, ADHD, anxiety, OCD, depression, and more.

Coleson, Nira. *Mental Health: Coping with PTSD*. Independently published, 2021.
Nearly 7 percent of Americans may experience post-traumatic stress disorder during their lives. Symptoms include reliving the event and anxiety. While most cases of PTSD occur in military veterans, it can happen to anyone after a disturbing traumatic event, such as a rape, an accident, or a sudden death of a loved one. Learn about how to cope with PTSD for a happier life.

Goldsmith, Connie. *Addiction and Overdose: Confronting an American Crisis*. Minneapolis: Twenty-First Century Books, 2018.
Drug overdose and death from both prescription painkillers and heroin are at epidemic highs in the United States. Meet the experts who study addiction. Hear stories of people with substance use disorders in recovery, and of loved ones left behind by those who died from an overdose. Learn about the connection between addiction and mental health disorders.

———. *Understanding Suicide: A National Epidemic*. Minneapolis: Twenty-First Century Books, 2017.
Suicide is among the top three causes of death for young people ages fifteen to twenty-four. This global epidemic claims forty-one thousand lives per year in the US alone. Suicide touches people of all ages, yet silence often surrounds these deaths, making suicide difficult to understand. Survivors' personal stories offer both grief and hope.

Peterson, Ashley L. *A Brief History of Stigma: Looking for Ways to Move beyond Mental Illness Stigma*. Mental Health @ Home Books, 2021. https://mentalhealthathome.org.
This book by a mental health nurse who lives with major depression explores the stigma of mental illness in three parts: What are stigma and stereotypes? Where and when do they occur? And how does one manage and reduce stigma?

Smith, Chuck, and Jason Hunt. *Understanding Addiction: Know Science, No Stigma*. N.p.: Visualize Publishing, 2021.
Drs. Smith and Hunt describe addiction as a disease, much like diabetes or a heart condition, and tells us why it needs to be treated that way. Their approach promises help for those personally struggling with addiction and for those who have a loved one suffering from addiction.

Stanford, Fatima Cody. *Facing Overweight and Obesity: A Complete Guide for Children and Adults*. Boston: MGH Psychiatry Academy, 2019.
Written by experts at Massachusetts General Hospital, this book combines medical information and counseling on being overweight, with a caring approach to the emotional aspects of living with weight-related conditions. Chapters cover the causes and dangers of obesity, along with examples of numerous lifestyle changes that one could make to prevent or reduce it.

Valens, C. L. *Domestic Violence Survivor Handbook: Steps to Freedom*. Independently published, 2021.
A survivor of intimate partner violence and stalking wrote this handbook. It provides easy-to-follow steps to help you identify if you are a victim and provides an informative guide on how to escape abuse and violence. It covers resources, how to stay hidden, and how to help others who have not yet escaped.

Volpe, John Della. *Fight: How Gen Z Is Channeling Their Fear and Passion to Save America*. New York: St. Martin's, 2022.
Gen Z, those born in the late 1990s to the early 2000s, are fighting back against serious societal problems, including the housing crisis, the opioid epidemic, school shootings, and global warming. They've organized around these issues, becoming more engaged than many older people and are willing to disrupt the status quo.

Wang, Esmé Weijun. *The Collected Schizophrenias*. Minneapolis: Graywolf, 2019.
The author of this book of essays tells her personal story of living with schizophrenia and how it affects her life. Her essays show what it's like to have this chronic mental health illness over many years and provide an inside look at the condition in an extraordinary way that can decrease stigma of the disease.

# Websites and Organizations

Centers for Disease Control and Prevention (CDC)

https://www.cdc.org

The CDC works to protect Americans from physical and mental health problems. Go to the main website and search for conditions from this book that you want to read more about, or any other physical or mental condition. Examples of offerings include numerous links to articles and statistics related to addiction (https://www.cdc.gov/pwid/addiction.html); sections on teen dating violence and risk factors for intimate partner violence (https://www.cdc.gov/violenceprevention/intimatepartnerviolence/); extensive information on mental health and mental illness, including a section on managing mental health during the pandemic and on "stress and coping resources" (https://www.cdc.gov/mentalhealth/index.htm); and pages of information and statistics on obesity, as well as ways to maintain healthy weight for all ages (https://www.cdc.gov/obesity/).

Mayo Clinic

https://www.mayoclinic.org/diseases-conditions/obesity/symptoms-causes/syc-20375742

The Mayo Clinic is a recognized national leader in providing health care and educating the public about it. The section on obesity offers pages of information on the causes and risk factors associated with it, the complications of obesity, and how obesity affects quality of life.

National Alliance on Mental Illness (NAMI)

https://nami.org/About-Mental-Illness

NAMI is a huge grassroots mental health organization that provides resources and information on such topics as warning signs and symptoms of mental illness, mental health conditions, treatment options, and stigma. Visit the NAMI website to learn about mental health, sign up for a fundraiser to help address mental health, or join the organization in its campaign to reduce mental health stigma.

National Alliance to End Homelessness

https://endhomelessness.org/

This nonprofit's website is a source of information on homelessness, including information on how it happens and to whom, solutions and statistics, and an up-to-date blog that covers many social and legal aspects of the unhoused at https://endhomelessness.org/blog/.

National Coalition Against Domestic Violence (NCADV)

https://ncadv.org/

This group works to fight intimate partner violence, to educate the public, and to support survivors. It discusses the dynamics of abuse, including why victims may stay in harmful relationships. The site includes a guide to teen dating violence at https://ncadv.org/blog/posts/quick-guide-teen-dating-violence.

National Equity Project

https://www.nationalequityproject.org/resources

This organization believes that all forms of prejudice and bias are learned and, therefore, can be unlearned. The resources page hosts discussions to help people understand how stigma and its subsequent oppression affects individuals and institutions. This site has articles, blog posts, podcasts, and videos about oppression, stigma, and equity.

National Institute on Drug Abuse (NIDA)

https://nida.nih.gov/

Part of the National Institutes of Health, NIDA is the leading federal agency supporting scientific research on drug use and its consequences. It provides detailed information on a dozen or more drugs—including alcohol—and the potential for the development of an addiction to each. It discusses drugs and the adolescent brain, as well as treatment and recovery.

Office on Women's Health

https://www.womenshealth.gov/

The US Department of Health and Human Services established this organization to improve the health of women and girls. Learn how issues such as date rape drugs, depression, intimate partner violence, and obesity affect women at https://www.womenshealth.gov/a-z-topics.

US Department of Veterans Affairs

https://www.ptsd.va.gov/understand/what/ptsd_basics.asp

This government site is dedicated to PTSD in veterans. It provides extensive information about PTSD, including the basic symptoms, statistics, information on understanding it, and how to get treatment. There are sections specifically for concerned family members and for health-care providers. It offers a sixteen-page downloadable booklet, *Understanding PTSD and PTSD Treatment*, at https://www.ptsd.va.gov/publications/print/understandingptsd_booklet.pdf/.

World Health Organization (WHO)

https://www.who.int/health-topics/mental-health

The WHO is an agency of the United Nations responsible for international public health. Its website has sections on stigma of many kinds. It provides many sections about mental health and mental illness. At https://www.who.int/health-topics/violence-against-women, you can learn how intimate partner violence affects woman not just in the US but in other countries.

World Obesity Federation

https://www.worldobesity.org/

This organization partners with the WHO to treat obesity across the globe. It supports research and education through studies and journals. It describes intervention that school and communities can take to manage obesity.

## Audio, Movies, and Videos

"*At Risk Summer* (Full Movie)." YouTube video, 1:15:17. Posted by e.E. Charlton-Trujillo, October 9, 2020. https://www.youtube.com/watch?v=X83mFR040hY. An author-filmmaker visits at-risk kids to encourage them to write about their experiences with stigma, bullying, rejection, and suicide attempts. The video contains appearances by authors Laurie Halse Anderson, Matt de la Peña, Ellen Hopkins, and others.

"Community Stories." San Francisco Project Access, 2019. https://www.sfprojectaccess.com/videos.html. This mental health organization's website features several videos of people talking about their struggles with mental illness. These include stories of people with PTSD and those who have experienced domestic violence and stigma as well. Stories vary in length but average twenty-five to thirty minutes.

"Peggy Portwine on Military Suicide." C-Span video, 7:12, July 10, 2014. https://www.c-span.org/video/?c4503154/peggy-portwine-military-suicide. In this video, Peggy Portwine testifies before Congress about her son's suicide and how the military needs to do a better job at helping veterans suffering from PTSD.

*Rebuilding Butte*. Lipp Studios. 25:26. https://amandalipp.com/lippstudios/tiny-home-film-project/. Amanda Lipp's film about an organization that built tiny homes for people after one of California's largest-ever wildfires has achieved national recognition and won awards. Natural disasters are one often overlooked reason that people become unhoused.

*Recovery Stories*. WISE—Wisconsin Initiative for Stigma Elimination, Rogers
    Behavioral Health, 2023. https://eliminatestigma.org/recovery-stories/.
    Select a story told by a real person from nine categories of mental illness,
    including anxiety, bipolar disorder, depression, and others, to learn about
    the person's experiences with recovery. The stories average four to
    five minutes.

"Stop the Stigma Video." YouTube video, 3:20. Posted by New Horizons
    Behavioral Health, September 18, 2015. https://www.youtube.com
    /watch?v=DWaOsPiv-gw.
    This is an award-winning public service announcement about stigma and how
    to stop it, prepared in conjunction with the CDC.

"Teen Brain Development." National Institute on Drug Abuse video, 3:10, March
    11, 2019. https://nida.nih.gov/videos/teen-brain-development.
    An intriguing video, it looks at the surprising and fascinating similarities
    between human brain development and computer programs.

# INDEX

## ABOUT THE AUTHOR

Connie Goldsmith has written more than twenty-five nonfiction books. Her books for young adult and middle-grade readers include subjects such as health topics, history, and military themes. She has also published more than two hundred magazine articles for adults and children. Her books include *Running on Empty: Sleeplessness in American Teens*; *Kiyo Sato: From a WWII Japanese Internment Camp to a Life of Service*; *Women in the Military: From Drill Sergeants to Fighter Pilots*; *Pandemic: How Climate, the Environment, and Superbugs Increase the Risk*; *Dogs at War: Military Canine Heroes*; and *Bombs over Bikini: the World's First Nuclear Disaster* (a Junior Library Guild Selection, a Children's Book Committee at Bank Street College Best Children's Book of the Year, and an SCBWI Crystal Kite winner). Goldsmith is a member of the Society of Children's Book Writers and Illustrators and the Authors Guild. She is a registered nurse with a bachelor of science degree in nursing and a master of public administration degree in health care. She lives near Sacramento, California.

## PHOTO ACKNOWLEDGMENTS

Image credits: Mitchell Leff/Getty Images, p. 6; Al Drago/Bloomberg/ Getty Images, p. 10; Courtesy of Amanda Lipp, p. 20; © Amanda Lipp, p. 21; SDI Productions/Getty Images, p. 29; Don Feria/AP Images for Each Mind Matters, p. 32; Chelsea Lauren/Getty Images, p. 36; Monkey Business Images/ Shutterstock, p. 37; Courtesy of Alisha Choquette, p. 40; Hyoung Chang/ MediaNews Group/The Denver Post/Getty Images, p. 52; © Joshua Marrone, pp. 58, 59, 60; sdecoret/Shutterstock, p. 72; The Creative Guy/Shutterstock, p. 78; SAUL LOEB/AFP/Getty Images, p. 87; SDI Productions/Getty Images, p. 90; Courtesy of Catherine Felt, p. 96; Icon Sportswire/Getty Images, p. 98; AP Photo/ The Journal-Star, Allison Hes, p. 100; Allen J. Schaben/Los Angeles Times/Getty Images, p. 105; David Paul Morris/Bloomberg/Getty Images, p. 115.

Cover and design elements: james weston/Shutterstock; Runrun2/Shutterstock; Natasha Barsova/Shutterstock; ex_artist/Shutterstock.